To Roger,

With my
very best wishes

London October 2015

# WINGS OF YOUTH

# Wings of Youth

*by*

HAROLD PREISKEL

The Memoir Club

© Harold Preiskel 2004

First published in 2004 by
The Memoir Club
Stanhope Old Hall
Stanhope
Weardale
County Durham

British Library Cataloguing in
Publication Data.
A catalogue record for this book
is available from the
British Library.

ISBN: 1 84104 112 2

Typeset by George Wishart & Associates, Whitley Bay.
Printed by CPI Bath.

*To the memory of my parents,*
*Lili and David Preiskel.*

# Foreword

## Wing Commander Andrew Brookes
*BA, MBA, MPhil, FRAeS, FRUSI, RAF (Ret'd)*
*Liveryman, Guild of Air Pilots and Air Navigators*

HAROLD PREISKEL and I were brought up in a time when flying was dangerous and sex was safe! Since then we have progressed in our separate ways – I to military reconnaissance and strike jet operations, and Harold to prosthodontics. But we are united in our love of, and empathy for, flying.

It is an old saying that only fools and birds fly, and birds don't fly at night. Moreover, birds are built for purpose whereas humans depend on technology to fly anywhere. When lounging in a jumbo jet cruising sedately above 30,000 ft., G & T in hand, it is hard to remember that flying is fundamentally about humans pitched against the elements. Harold takes us from the Auster Aiglet to the Cessna Citation, from clipping the treetops to 41,000 ft. When Harold is on his Mediterranean capers, or risking hitting an iceberg around Greenland, he captures the fear and thrill of flying that combines to form the basis of real aviation.

*Wings of Youth* is a tale well told for three reasons. First, there are no pictures of dodgy teeth in it. Second, in the video age where everything seems to be done quickly, it is lovely to be transported back to a bygone age of Miles

Messengers, Croydon days and navigating by following railway lines. Third, for all the scent of Biggles and Gypsy Moth engines, Harold does not gloss over the fact that aircraft can kill. There are still challenges out there that need to be faced professionally. As the saying goes, there are old pilots and bold pilots, but there are no old, bold pilots. Harold proves that the wise aviator is someone who knows his aircraft, his weather forecast and his limitations.

For its readability and evocative canter through a fascinating and fulfilling life of aviation, I commend this book to you. Enjoy!

*Andrew Brookes*

# Acknowledgements

Without the enthusiasm, typing skills, and organisational abilities of Elsie Crook and Linda Nancekievill this project could not have been contemplated.

I am also indebted to Gillian Lee, working outside her normal field of medical illustration, for her help with the cover, the artwork, and all the illustrations.

To Tom Sampson of the Croydon Airport Society, to Ian Briggs of Luton Airport and to Flight International, my thanks for the loan of illustrations. I am also indebted to Jacky Taylor of Ambrion Aviation and to Paul Loveday and Dave Macready of the Vintage Aircraft Club for their photographs.

To those who have read the proofs and given advice, my humble thanks.

Finally, to the staff of The Memoir Club, my appreciation of their professional skills in bringing the project to reality.

# Contents

# Illustrations

After this era of great pilots is gone, as the era of great sea captains has gone — each nudged aside by the march of inventive genius, by steel caps and copper discs and hair-thin wires on white faces that are dumb, but speak – it will be found I think that all the science of flying has been captured in the breadth of an instrument board, but not the religion of it.

**Beryl Markham, 1935**

# Introduction

THE STIMULUS for this book came from the President of our Students' Union who persuaded me to give a talk on my early experiences in aviation. It concerns an era of aviation that is past, long past, yet still lives on. The paradox may be explained by the number of pilots who fly the most sophisticated aircraft for their profession, and the most basic for their pleasure. If you still look skyward on hearing an aircraft the text will interest you.

In the 1950s the world's first jet powered airliners were being built in the United Kingdom while a few miles away the pilots of the future were being trained to fly in open cockpit biplanes. I was one of them and this book is an account of my first 100 hours or so as a fledgling pilot together with some later experiences. Our instructors had survived World War II and a difficult transition into civilian life. A zeal for the magic of flight burnt within and it was this enthusiasm that they, in turn, imparted to their pupils. Given a modicum of provocation they would produce heart-stopping displays of outstanding flying skill, demonstrations that no student would ever forget.

While the performance and handling of modern aircraft bear little resemblance to those of days gone by, the principles of powered flight have not changed. In a similar vein, the electronic age has revolutionised cockpit management and navigational skills while human behaviour patterns remain doggedly constant. Basic airmanship does not alter.

To those who complain that the text merely serves to illustrate examples of irresponsibility I can only plead youth and the statute of limitations. I would also claim that it records a period of aviation that exists no more but from which there are still important lessons to learn today. A few names have been changed but the anecdotes are accurate insofar as I can recall.

# Chapter 1

# The Lure of Flight

THE GENTLE CHUGGING of the Gypsy Major aero engine enhances the joy of a beautiful spring evening. Below, the English countryside with its neat hedgerows and cultivated fields is resplendent in the setting sun, but gleaming patches of waterlogged fields remind me that not all days are like this. Each village and town appears to be holding an open air fête, brave testimony to the British public with its never ending faith in the weather. Ahead, an event has just finished and I look down on a kaleidoscopic patchwork of cars in an enclosure as they move like a disordered platoon towards a hopelessly narrow exit. Unbeknown to the drivers the winding lane outside is utterly clogged. Above, I float in complete unfettered freedom. Stately country homes hidden from prying eyes hold no secrets from the air, neither do tennis courts, swimming pools, cricket pitches, woods, rolling hills, streams and rivers that contribute to the beauty of the land.

A slight forward movement of the throttle, a dip of the nose and the chugging of the motor assumes a more urgent tone. My fifty year-old Chipmunk gathers speed as the controls become taut and wind noise intrudes.

Gentle easing back of the control column and the horizon turns blue. Engine and wind noise quieten as for a few brief seconds we defy gravity and soar heavenwards – but not for

*Chipmunks in formation.*

long. Over my head a greenish brown tinge appears as the horizon comes into view upside down. For an instant there is silence as the wind dies away; now we are gathering speed and a crescendo of noise as the nose drops earthwards with the countryside dead ahead. I apply firm backward pressure on the control column and I am compressed into my seat as the earth begins to return to its usual position. Now the nose rises once again and I hold it in its position on the horizon as the column is moved across to the right together with opposite rudder and the world rotates. A slight forward movement of the column holds the nose in the correct position and I feel myself falling until the straps bite into my thighs and shoulders. Above my head cows graze peacefully, oblivious of the Chipmunk. The engine splutters, unhappy with the lack of gravity, and the earth continues to rotate now with changed rudder. As if to welcome the country back

*Harold beside the Chipmunk in recent times.*

into place the Gypsy Major bursts into full song with an apology for its previous cough. To my right the fiery tinge to the clouds and the timeless tranquillity of the world from above bring back memories of earlier flights and adventures. Not all were so beautiful nor so tranquil.

As all pilots know, the transition from boredom to terror can take but the blink of an eyelid, a fact I was about to rediscover. Many a pilot of an earlier era can attest that when cruising serenely at 10,000 ft. nothing can spoil the day more effectively than the unexpected arrival of a 12,000 ft. mountain. In my case I knew exactly where I was over Central France where the ground reached up to 4,000 ft. I was flying a modern small twin-engine aircraft from London to the South of France on a route I knew well. Cruising at 9,000 ft. there was little to worry about – or so I thought. The weather forecast was fair with occasional light showers

on the way. Lulled into a false sense of security engendered
by an uncannily accurate autopilot that deviated neither from
its assigned heading nor from its assigned altitude I could
afford to relax and enjoy the changing cloudscape with just
the radio to keep me busy. In and out of cumulus we
plunged from lightness to darkness every few minutes with
bumps and small thumps as we penetrated the changing air
currents of the clouds. The temperature was well above
freezing so there were no ice problems to consider. Small
wonder that I did not notice that the clouds were becoming
darker and the bumps somewhat more pronounced.

Thwack! As if hit by a rifle shot the little aircraft bucked
violently, my feet left the rudder pedals, charts and pencils
flew around the cabin and I hit my head on the roof. The
transition from relaxation to a fight for survival had taken
but a few seconds: just about the time it took for me to
realise what had happened. I had blundered into a violent
thunderstorm hidden amongst the other clouds. Of course I
had flown through many a storm before. Some flexed the
wings and many threw the cockpit contents around and
made the passengers scream but this was like no storm I had
ever encountered. The turbulence was beyond anything I
had ever imagined let alone experienced. The aircraft was
out of my control. Hypnotised by the instruments that had
all gone crazy I began to realise that this was a battle I might
not win. It was strange, but after the initial terrifying shock I
was no longer frightened – just resigned to the inevitable.
Stranger still, I had the impression that I had trespassed into
the domain of a malevolent giant who was now bent on
murder. Turbulence was no description for the hammering
that was shaking my eyes in their sockets and was tearing the

aircraft apart. I could not even change radio frequency without risking pulling the radio out of its panel. No civil aircraft could take this form of punishment. It was as if the giant storm was extracting vengeance for my intrusion. The fact that the intrusion was unintentional had no bearing on the penalty.

Demonstrating my helplessness and the puny power of machines made by man it effortlessly sucked me heavenwards, throttles closed, at more than twice the rate of climb the aircraft could ever achieve at full power. I could only stare disbelievingly as the altimeter dizzily wound up and the rate of climb indicator hit its stops while bracing myself for the inevitable downdraught that would follow. The upward rush was carrying the aircraft towards the freezing level, and there was no chance that its limited de-icing equipment could cope with severe icing. I even began to worry about lack of oxygen as the lift-like ascent continued, but not for long. Seconds later I was in a cauldron of seething water, assailed by piercing crackling sounds as if the aircraft was being hosed down with ball bearings. Then came the sledgehammer blows of hail that threatened to smash the windscreen and puncture the aircraft skin, while a cacophony of noise like a hundred machine guns almost drowned out the occasional blaring of the stall warning horn. The straps bit into my skin, and I banged my head on the roof again and yet again. I was fighting a losing battle. Suddenly, there was a stunning, blinding, yellow green flash and a burning smell that numbed my senses until I realised it was a lightning strike. The Twin Comanche was built for aerodynamic efficiency rather than strength. It was amazing that nothing had broken yet, but for how long could the plane hold together? I was doing my best to minimise control inputs but feared that the instrument gyros might tumble in the extreme attitudes to which the aircraft was being thrown. Without the gyro instruments there was no chance of keeping even the semblance of control in these conditions with just limited blind flying instruments. Disorientation would be inevitable followed by loss of control and a rapid speed build-up leading to structural failure. I wondered if the tail or a wing would fail first.

I gave up hope. All I could do was to attempt to hold the aircraft in the correct attitude while the airspeed fluctuated wildly. In desperation I asked Air Traffic for assistance as I needed to know the extent of the storm and the best way out. Paris Air Traffic claimed they could not see the storm on their radar. They could not believe it was impossible to change radio frequency but did complain that I was not maintaining my assigned height. My terse reply that it was a miracle that I was still above the ground did not improve relationships. I wondered what friends and family would say when they heard of the crash. I thought I heard, 'He just had this madness for flying, such a shame.' Then it was over!

The giant became tired of playing like a cat with a mouse, and simply threw me out into crystal clear air. Ahead lay the hills of the Massif Central, wet and glistening in the summer sunshine. Behind, an angry ermine shrouded thundercloud spread its venom high towards the stratosphere. Gingerly, I first checked the aircraft and then myself for damage. We both bore scars but mine were relatively superficial. I am not going to fly again without weather radar, I promised myself.

As I nursed the aircraft towards a diversion at Lyon I had a strange thought.

'What on earth am I doing here?' I mused. I was to ask myself the same question during a North Atlantic crossing.

# CHAPTER 2

# Westward Bound

A FEW YEARS LATER I found myself gazing at an endless sea of ice. Slowly, laboriously and painfully an ant worked its way across a mountainous football pitch. The ant was black, ink black, but the pitch was blinding white, white tinged with hues of blue and green. The ant was the shadow of our beloved Twin Comanche, the pitch the awe-inspiring never-ending mass of the Greenland ice plateau. An immense feeling of loneliness swept by as I contemplated the route from London and the hazards ahead of my first Atlantic crossing from east to west against the prevailing wind.

Stephen, my invariably optimistic and cheerful partner with the aircraft, had telephoned me some two weeks before:

'Can you take the plane to Rochester?'

Rochester in Kent was some twenty minutes flying time from our base at Leavesden, just north-west of London. It meant skirting around the northern and eastern suburbs of London, crossing the river Thames and river Medway.

'No problem,' I replied.

'Excellent,' said Stephen. 'Now that you've agreed I hope you realise our destination is not Rochester, Kent, but Rochester, New York!'

In those few moments the decision was made to fly the North Atlantic.

*The Twin Comanche.*

The Twin Comanche had an excellent range for a light twin-engine aircraft but North Atlantic distances were vast. Few, if any, diversions were possible and this was going to take careful analysis of weather forecasts. Although the Twin Comanche could fly 1,200 miles it did not carry the specialist navigation and communication equipment required when the nearest radio station might be several hundred miles away. We were going to be reliant on good old-fashioned dead reckoning and fend for ourselves. Global Positioning Systems using satellites had yet to be invented. We would be out of range of radio navigation aids for many hundreds of miles. We were also going to be out of touch with any air traffic controller. Another missing feature was toilet facilities, requiring careful preparation before a flight of six hours duration or more!

Navigation was further complicated by the extremely large

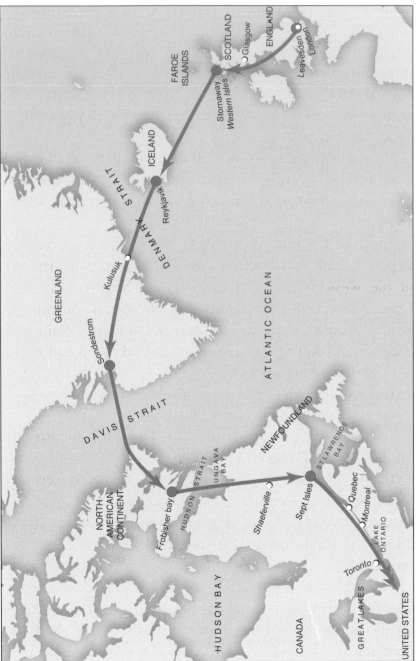

*Our route from Leavesden, London to the USA.*

magnetic variation to be found over certain sections of the route. Then there was the ever fickle weather which could change at a moment's notice. Suitable fuel was only available at certain airfields and very expensive. Apart from our normal safety equipment, we felt it prudent to take with us immersion suits with suitable radio transmitters and survival packs – just in case!

The route we selected took into account the availability of fuel, interest, overnight accommodation, and the fact that one vital airfield on the shortest line was closed at week-ends.

The first leg took us some 600 miles from Leavesden airport, on the northern outskirts of London, to Stornaway in the Western Isles, off the coast of Scotland. We left Leavesden on one of the hottest days of the year and enjoyed beautiful weather up to the Lake District. Crossing the border into Scotland, we ran into the solid cloud and heavy rain that had been forecast.

'It always rains in Scotland,' grinned Stephen.

'Only when I'm on holiday,' I smiled.

We bounced our way across the unseen hills beneath us until we passed Glasgow.

'Echo Romeo, the instrument landing system at Stornaway, is now unserviceable,' an anxious air traffic controller called. 'The weather is wind 240/25 knots, 2 km visibility in rain and 8 octas at 400 ft., what are your intentions?'

I was about to reply 'Honourable' but suddenly realised why the controller was anxious. The weather there was right on the limits of the minimum requirements for the non-precision landing aid that was the only one now available. It would have been easy to divert to Glasgow, but we knew that the next leg from Stornaway to Iceland was likely to be made against headwinds. For obvious reasons it was better to shorten this leg.

'Go for it,' agreed Stephen, as we decided to attempt to land at Stornaway and, if this proved impossible, then to return to Glasgow.

'You'd better get it right,' muttered Stephen, looking at the approach charts. 'There are hills all around.'

The beacon was about four miles from the runway. We crossed in thick cloud and heavy rain, started the stop watch, and I concentrated on the descent.

At 400 ft. we were still in cloud, then, 'I've got the field,' called Stephen. The blanket lifted from the windscreen and there, not quite on the nose, stretched the soaked runway. On the right the hills disappeared ominously into the overcast.

We had left Leavesden with a temperature of about 25°C. We landed in wind, rain, low cloud and a temperature of about 7°C. We hastily grabbed our anoraks before leaving the aircraft.

The sector from Stornaway to Reykjavik was the longest over-water section of the journey, around 700 miles, and we calculated that we could safely accept a headwind of 20 knots. To the north of our track lay the Faroe Islands to which we could divert if the wind slowed us too much – provided the weather there was good enough for landing. If not, we would have to return to Stornaway. All this required calculations to establish our various decision points. Another factor was to allow for the possible loss of one engine. The aircraft would fly more slowly on one engine and it would require further calculations to cover this eventuality. In fact, the forecast looked quite reasonable, for the North Atlantic at least, with a light headwind expected.

Shortly after lunch found us airborne into the low cloud and rain; twenty minutes later we broke out into the brilliant sunshine on top of the layer of cloud and made contact with Scottish radar. Wind drift had to be very carefully calculated and an allowance made for the rapidly changing magnetic field as we flew north-west. Half an hour later we finally lost contact with Scottish radio control and could no longer receive the beacon that had helped us plot our initial drift and speed.

'Lonely?' I asked.

It was an eerie feeling to be alone, knowing that around you there was nothing but the vast expanse of the Atlantic Ocean and, to the north, the Faroe Islands.

After an hour we encountered substantial clouds and periods of quite heavy rain followed by sunshine. Then we saw water as the cloud broke up, endless empty sea. Our calculations showed the headwind to be weaker than forecast but also coming from a slightly different direction, probably owing to the movement of the low pressure system that had been centred over Iceland.

One of the pleasant features of the aviation community is the international co-operation between pilots. In the case of the North Atlantic, over-flying airliners will usually relay messages to the controlling centres and it is always comforting to be able to talk to somebody. Called a TWA jumbo, 'Echo Romeo, we've passed on your position report. The weather is clearing in Iceland. Have a nice day!'

After two or more hours of inactivity we were relieved to

see the navigation instruments began to flicker and then come to life. We were more or less on track.

The TWA Boeing pilot was correct and the cloud broke up as we approached Iceland. We were able to speak to Iceland control about a hundred miles out. Reykjavik seemed anxious about position reports – puzzling in such a vast empty area. Our first landfall was over a small volcanic island that featured a semi-circular wall of granite 1,000 feet high surrounding a village, and about twenty minutes later we crossed the coast of Iceland. The airfield at Reykjavik appeared to be in the middle of the town and close to the sea.

'Welcome to Reykjavik,' grinned the handling agent sporting a thick yellow anorak. He pointed to the pale streaks of sunlight penetrating a thin layer of high cloud. 'You've chosen a nice warm summer day for your arrival, it's nearly 6 degrees,' he smiled.

We telephoned the air traffic office.

'Welcome, did you enjoy the crossing?' boomed a cheerful voice.

'It was interesting, thank you, but why were you so anxious about position reports – we must have been the only aircraft at our altitude within hundreds of miles,' I answered.

'Don't be too sure,' came the answer. 'Before the war there were only two aircraft in Iceland and they managed to collide on the airfield.'

Reykjavik was an attractive small town with a strong Danish influence. The volcanic activity was taken for granted and used for heating homes. None of the inhabitants appeared to be surprised when steam could be seen rising from the centres of lawns on roundabouts! The other

surprising feature was that even after we had finished a
splendid dinner around midnight, it was still light.

Sunday morning started with a major crisis. The weather
forecast showed quite good weather from Iceland to
Greenland across 500 miles of sea, the Denmark Strait.
However, there was an occluded front containing vicious
weather coming towards the far side of Greenland
approaching our destination, Sondestrom, which lay at the
end of a long fjord on the western side of Greenland. This
meant that we had to cross the Denmark Strait and then
the entire width of the ice plateau before reaching the
airfield. Greenland virtually closed on a Sunday and
Sondestrom was the only airfield open other than in an
emergency. Sondestrom was more than five hours flying
away and if the weather closed it down just before we arrived
we would have no fuel to go anywhere else. This provided
food for thought.

'Let's look at Kulusuk,' I suggested. 'It's a small gravel strip
off the east coast of Greenland. If the weather is reasonable
we could land in an emergency even if we have to sleep in
the plane. It opens tomorrow and we can buy fuel then.'

Stephen raised his eyebrows. 'OK with me!'

Once we had passed Kulusuk and crossed the Greenland
coast we would no longer be able to return to Iceland. The
problem was that Kulusuk was fogbound as our take-off time
approached. Would the fog clear in the three hours it would
take us to cross the Denmark Strait?

'Let's give it a whirl,' I suggested.

The weather was brilliantly clear yet the ocean stretched
forever. I thought of World War II and the fateful encounter

between the *Bismarck* and the *Hood* in these freezing waters more than forty years earlier.

'How on earth did the ships find each other?' I thought aloud.

'Look at the visibility,' came the reply.

We could see forever but there was nothing to be seen. For two hours we droned across the water; then I saw land. A faint smudge appeared on the horizon.

'I can see Greenland,' I called.

'Impossible, we've nearly two hundred miles to run; you can't see that far from 10,000 ft.'

'But there are mountains on the coast.'

We both stared at the horizon. There could be no doubt. Slowly but surely a faint line of mountains could be discerned so far away that we did not appear to be moving. Then the sea itself began to change character. Small specks of white became larger.

'The sea is freezing,' Stephen exclaimed.

By now the mountainous Greenland coast was clearly visible and we were flying over packed ice. Occasionally we saw scattered icebergs, some with their own mountains and valleys. They even appeared to contain their own green lakes.

'Why doesn't that water freeze as well?' I mused.

The coastline kept our attention. From sea level it rose sharply in a jagged series of upward curves to the ice plateau 9,000 ft. high. To the north of our track gleaming mountains stretched skyward, and just off the nose lay our diversion Kulusuk under a blanket of fog. The fog was quite thin and patches of sea and land could be seen.

'Another hour and it will be clear,' I murmured.

In answer to our anxious query a PanAm pilot called,

'Echo Romeo, we've passed on your position report. The west coast of Greenland is still clear and the front is 100 miles off the coast. You should be fine. Good luck!'

The decision was made. We donned our oxygen masks and began our climb to 13,000 ft. The Twin Comanche could not maintain 9,000 ft. if we were to lose an engine but at least it would descend slowly. The additional, 4000 ft. gave us a cushion that might allow us to reach one coast or the other.

The mountains of the coast gave way to the vastness of the ice plateau, a white desert 300 miles wide and 1,000 miles long. Against the brilliance of the ice cap it was hard to make out details but ridges, precipitous ravines and the occasional hill could be seen. Strange, iridescent turquoise and green hues emanated from sections of the awe-inspiring panorama – and nothing moved, apart from our shadow. In the middle of this spectacular desolation two radar stations had been built with the unlikely names of Sob Story and Sea Bass. They formed part of a military radar chain. Stephen called them on the radio.

'What do you folks do in your free time?' Stephen grinned.

'We play golf on the world's longest and least crowded course!'

'But how do you find the balls?' I enquired.

'We use red balls – sorry, folks, we can't chat now as we're busy. Have a nice one,' drawled a Texan voice.

We wondered what on earth could keep them so busy in their desolation, then we had our own work to consider as we neared the western edge of the plateau. The sky still seemed to be clear.

Greenland's western coast resembled Norway. An army of

mountains stretched towards the sea separated by finger-like fjords running their irregular course inland towards the ice plateau. As they reached the base of the plateau the ends of the fjords were marked by almost vertical walls of rock. Our destination, Sondestrom, was situated at the inland end of the Sondestrom fjord some 85 miles long. The ground fell sharply from the edge of the plateau down to Sondestrom at sea level. We slid down between the mountains into the fjord. Although the fjord was wide enough to turn the Twin Comanche there didn't seem a great deal of room to spare. The single runway appeared surrounded by three vertical walls.

'Fancy landing here in instrument conditions?' I enquired. Stephen's expression did not require words.

Sondestrom served as a military base and civil aerodrome. The only means of transport was by sea and air. There were roads but they only joined nearby villages. Fortunately, the aerodrome had a comfortable hostel. In the evening there was nothing to do except to talk with other visiting pilots and drink beer – in vast quantities. We learnt that if you obeyed the rules even quite large commercial aircraft could be operated from the base. However, the first time you broke the rules would also be the last time.

Next morning I awoke to the hissing of rain on the windows; the front had arrived. The local time was 04.00 but since it had been light all night it was difficult to judge. I looked out of the window to see the aircraft surrounded by small lakes of water. Low cloud scudded up the fjord obliterating the surrounding mountains and providing a general air of gloom.

A council of war was held over breakfast following a visit to the weather office. The front stretched about a hundred miles westwards across the mountains with clear weather behind over the sea. The problem was that the front was slow moving and would take many hours to clear Sondestrom.

'I see three possibilities,' I said. 'We lose a day and wait here, or we fly low level down the fjord until we are clear of the weather, or climb through the cloud and fly at a safe height.'

'If we wait we'll run the risk of Frobisher going down as there is a second front approaching it,' answered Stephen.

'Don't even think of scud running down the fjord,' said a local pilot. 'You risk coming to a sudden halt.'

'Against what?'

'Against a rock face, if the visibility suddenly drops. Near the sea you might even hit an iceberg.'

'I hadn't thought of that,' Stephen muttered, 'We don't have too many icebergs in the English Channel.'

'Talking about ice, how much do you think we'll pick up if we climb on top?' I asked.

'Let's go and ask the pilot of the Dash-7 that's just landed.'

The rain-soaked tarmac was not at all inviting. The tail section of the Dash-7 had been roped off to avoid ice from the high T-shaped tail falling onto the disembarking passengers.

'Welcome aboard,' the captain smiled. 'The tops are about 7,000 ft. – I don't think you will have too much trouble.'

'That's what we'll do,' I replied. 'Better be familiar with the instrument approach charts here just in case we have to turn back.'

'Remember your question yesterday about approaching Sondestrom in bad weather?' smiled Stephen.

'But that was yesterday!' I grinned and so the decision was made.

The murky airfield did not invite take-off and we spent time checking our calculations.

'The magnetic variation is 46°,' Stephen announced.

In Britain it was about 7°. Since the wind aloft was forecast relative to True North this required rechecking the calculations.

'I hope the de-icing equipment copes,' I called as I opened the throttles.

Our friendly pilot was correct with his advice. We picked up a small amount of ice before we broke into the blinding sunlight above. On either side mountain peaks poked menacingly through the cloud tops. At 10,000 ft. we were well above the cloud and so could admire the vista. Exactly as forecast the cloud began to break as we approached the coast leaving the front behind us.

By now we had become accustomed to the wonders of nature but the sight that lay ahead took our breath away.

'Just look at that,' was all that Stephen could utter.

The Davis Strait, the sea to the west of Greenland, was frozen. Spectacular icebergs sailed like stately galleons reflecting hues of blue and green. This white-tinged vista stretched to a never-ending horizon while behind us the mountains projected through their mantles of cloud. There were no reliable radio aids in the area so it was a question of dead reckoning for some 300 miles across the frozen ocean to our first landfall on the North American continent. Cape Dyer on Baffin Island was another lonely radar outpost and the helpful operator seemed glad of the opportunity to talk to someone.

'Have a nice day,' were his parting words, as we crossed the barren coastline almost on track and entered the North American Continent. There were still hours flying across desolation before we reached our destination, Frobisher Bay. The airfield boasted an impressive runway, a small terminal, and very little else. We landed after a four-hour flight from Sondestrom. This was the first occasion on which we were asked to produce our passports.

The man who refuelled our aircraft kindly took us into town to buy some lunch. Apart from one or two modern buildings, 'town' appeared something out of a Wild West film. The ground was permafrost, there were no paved roads, and most of the houses were wood and built on stilts. Dust and insects blew everywhere. Voracious mosquitoes attacked everything that moved.

'If you think this is bad, try the winter,' our guide said, 'It's so cold that if you don't hangar the aircraft as soon as you land you have to leave it here!' he grinned.

All the locals eagerly anticipated the first fall of snow, expected in early September, as this put an end to the mosquito attacks. The United States and Canadian governments appeared to support a population of 1,000 who were, in turn, meant to look after 1,500 Eskimos. Everything from food to fuel had to be brought in by air, or sea when the water was navigable.

'Fancy a night here?' I enquired.

'Definitely not!' replied Stephen.

'OK, let's check the weather.'

From Frobisher our track lay more than 1,000 miles due

south, to a point near the mouth of the river St. Laurence, Sept-Îles. This was going to take about six hours. The weather forecast was far from good with heavy cloud over the southern part of the route.

Our destination, Sept-Îles, was closed by bad weather but a slight improvement was forecast. However, unlike the earlier legs we had the luxury of two diversion airfields en route should the weather not get better. We bade farewell to Arctic latitudes and turned southwards across the frozen Hudson Strait to make our landfall on the mainland of Canada. An enormous bay, the Ungava Bay, lay on our route. It is about 150 miles long but is dwarfed by its neighbour the Hudson Bay. Two hours from Frobisher we crossed a small outpost of civilisation, Fort Chimo, which boasted an airport. The snow had given way to tundra and we began to see lakes that were not frozen. As we progressed southwards navigation became more conventional and we could rely on radio beacons.

'Back to civilisation,' I grinned.

'Yes, but look at the weather.'

The weather had deteriorated and radio reports showed Sept-Îles was still closed owing to low cloud and poor visibility. The alternate airport, Shaeferville, was still open – just. We monitored the weather every half hour.

By now we were flying in clear sky, in bright sunshine, but only just above a continual layer of cloud. It was hard to believe that underneath us it was not only night, but a dark wet one as well. The transition from a bright and sparkling environment into a murky overcast is spectacular and it never ceases to amaze me however many times I make the change. Two hours later the weather had slightly improved.

'Tell you what,' I said. 'We should now be able to get into Sept-Îles but if we can't we still have enough fuel to get back to Shaeferville or one of the other St. Laurence airports, OK?'

We over-flew Shaeferville and set course for Sept-Îles.

'Echo Romeo, cleared for procedural ILS, descent to 2,000 ft. and call the localiser established,' called the controller.

'They're not offering much help,' muttered Stephen.

'They're too busy,' I laughed. We couldn't hear radio from another plane in the sky. We crossed the radio beacon, started our stopwatch then dutifully turned inbound. The instrument landing system showed we were aligned with the runway.

'Echo Romeo localizer established.'

'Echo Romeo cleared to descend on the ILS, you are number one.'

We sank further into the damp murk.

'I've got the lights,' called Stephen, as the welcoming approach lights appeared like magic out of the gloom. More than six hours had passed since Frobisher as our wheels touched the rain-swept runway of Sept-Îles.

The dampness of the night melted in the warmth of the reception we received from local controllers and fuellers, who were somewhat surprised to find a foreign aircraft flying around in such miserable skies, and were particularly happy to discover that both pilots spoke French. The fueller became so carried away that in his enthusiasm he filled not only the tanks but splashed a generous excess onto the wings. We retired for a much needed sleep.

The next morning proved bright and cheerful, but the

news from the efficient met officer was not so good – a line
of storms was forecast along our route between Quebec and
Montreal.

The weather for the Great Lakes was expected to be good
if we could penetrate a possible line of thunderstorms – and
I now had great respect for these monsters.

Shortly after take-off from Sept-Îles we realised that one
of our six fuel tanks was leaking. Since we had ample fuel for
the flight our main concern was to empty the leaking tank as
fast as possible and trim the plane before we encountered
any rough weather. Through the clouds we had the
occasional glimpse of the massive St. Laurence River.

An hour out from Sept-Îles the clouds began to get
thicker and darken, the intensity of the rain increased, and
we began to feel the high frequency shudders that mark the
proximity of thunderclouds. Instinctively we braced
ourselves but the radar operators at Quebec directed us
round the worst of the turbulence and, once clear of
Montreal, we began to see patches of blue with large
cumulus clouds stretching up around us. By the time we
approached Lake Ontario the weather was beautiful. Lake
Ontario is a truly great lake – from 8,000 feet it is quite
difficult to see the opposite shore. Now was the time we
entered United States airspace.

We had considerable problems persuading Boston Air
Traffic Centre (sorry, Center) that we really were British and
not Canadian. The British registrations start with a 'G'
(Golf), the Canadian with a 'C' (Charlie). We had even more
difficulty in Rochester, New York, where the customs officer
only appeared to have heard of London, Ontario. He misread
the 'G' on the side of the aircraft for the 'C' that he saw

every day and could not make sense of what we were trying to tell him.

'Sir, do you have fruit, fresh vegetables or have you visited a farm recently?' he enquired.

'No, we are importing this aircraft back to the USA.'

'Sir, I asked you if you had obtained fresh vegetables, fruit or had visited a farm,' he persisted.

'No Sir,' we replied – we gave up on the aircraft!

The inescapable facts were that we were in North America, and the journey had been truly memorable. Why had I not done this years before?

'This guy really doesn't seem interested in the aircraft,' said Stephen.

'Now don't get me into any more trouble with the Customs, just remember Cranfield,' I smiled. We both laughed.

A month or two earlier we had rented an eight-seater Piper Navajo to fly ourselves from London to Paris with Stephen's collection of dresses for the next season – Stephen being in the fashion business when he was not flying. The Navajo was based at Cranfield, an airfield about sixty miles north of London that does not normally have Customs and so we had arranged for a Customs Officer to supervise our departure. We found the van containing the dress collection and after a search found the aircraft which looked rather well worn and didn't fill either of us with great confidence.

We climbed the stairs to the control tower where a friendly gentleman behind the desk told us that the Customs Officer hadn't arrived yet but that we might as well put in the flight plan. Neither of us were in a hurry as we wanted plenty of time to check the aircraft and to load it with several hundred dresses. Returning to the control tower we found nothing much had changed except for mild panic as a visiting aircraft from Germany had managed to get itself not only lost but short of fuel and the controllers were bringing it in towards Cranfield. There were two or three other pilots listening in to the radio and an elderly gentleman in a tweed jacket with leather patches sleeping in an armchair completely uninterested in the activity around him. The plane eventually made a safe landing and two rather shaken German pilots were brought up to the control tower.

'You must stay here until the Customs and Immigration have examined you,' said the controller. 'But please have a cup of coffee while you wait.'

The pilots looked as though a whisky or a double brandy might have been more appropriate but said nothing.

'While you're waiting you had better fill up these Customs forms,' said the controller. The two pilots sat down at a table with a pen and a strange puzzled look came over their faces.

'Vee do not know the enchin serial number, ver eeze it?' asked the captain.

Stephen, always one to be helpful in such situations, sauntered over to the table.

'Don't worry about the numbers,' he smiled, 'Just put down your telephone numbers – that will keep the Customs happy.'

Out of the corner of my eye I saw old leather-patches stir from his armchair; at least he was alive. Then he spoke. 'I don't think that is a very good idea,' he said.

'Why not?' said Stephen. 'I have been flying for many

years and I have never had any trouble – probably the Customs Officers can't even read,' he smiled.

'Are you trying to tell me my job?' said old leather-patches, who was well and truly awake by now and did not look at all amused.

'Of course not,' said Stephen. 'In any case what is your job?'

'I am the Customs Officer,' replied leather-patches. 'And what is more I intend to examine every one of the four hundred dresses that you have just loaded into your aircraft.'

He certainly had the last laugh and we departed for Paris about two and a half hours late.

I saw no reason why the United States Customs Officers should have any better sense of humour than those in Great Britain. 'Whatever you do,' I muttered to Stephen, 'don't upset the officer this time.' In fact the Customs Officer turned out to be absolutely charming and very helpful, but not the slightest bit interested in the aircraft.

# CHAPTER 3

# First Steps

FROM A VERY EARLY AGE I had been fascinated by aircraft. I simply failed to grow up in this respect. I was an avid reader of adventure stories, particularly those involving flying, and like most small boys I had my heroes all of whom were pilots. At holiday times I would admire gulls and their ability to soar with consummate ease along the cliffs of the South Coast and soon began to appreciate the invisible currents of air that they sought with such apparent lack of effort. While appreciating the wonders of nature it was the production of man-made flying machines that held the greatest fascination. It was not long before I became a keen, if somewhat inexpert, builder of model aircraft. In my hands gliders and rubber-powered models suffered an alarming accident rate.

Flight profiles often resembled a ballistic trajectory culminating in a heap of crumpled balsa wood. Sometimes the models flew too well and disappeared out of sight. Occasionally the magnetic attraction of treetops was the cause of the mishap. All told this was a thoroughly unsatisfactory state of affairs that led to my interest in models that flew in circles with a life expectancy of more than one flight. It was not long before the peace and quiet of my parents' home in north-west London was shattered by the tortured scream of model aero engines. Noisy flying objects tethered by control lines circled at ridiculous speeds around our narrow garden while the pilot in the middle did his best not to become giddy. The accident rate improved even if relationships with our neighbours suffered. In retrospect I am surprised that we received only the occasional complaint. The noisy adventures in the garden surprised more than our neighbours. They amazed visitors to our home which was well known for classical music and academic pursuits such as chess in which I played active roles. Somewhere, there was an errant gene.

I was able to pursue my interest in aviation at school where we had an active Cadet Corps. We did our share of square-bashing, dismantled and reassembled ancient weapons, and learnt the rudiments of fieldcraft. Eventually we began to learn something about aircraft. As cadets we took ourselves seriously. We were subjected to military type discipline and took pride in our spit and polish. We even began to think of ourselves as airmen. In fact, we were probably mischievous spoilt brats but we were always made welcome at the RAF Stations that we visited.

I cannot say that our behaviour was exemplary, particularly during our annual camps. I vividly remember an occasion on which an RAF Flight Sergeant, well known for his belligerent manner, was ordered to supervise us at night to prevent the usual nocturnal pranks. He positioned his desk at the foot of the open centre staircase. Behind him stood the regulation fire extinguishers and fire buckets. From his vantage point downstairs he had a good view of most of the corridors and little movement was possible without his knowledge. This was going to be a quiet night, or so he thought.

Hours later his harassed voice was overheard telephoning a disbelieving Duty Office: 'Fire! Fire! Send urgent assistance. The fire bucket is blazing!'

Unbeknown to him one of our squad had surreptitiously dropped a small amount of lithium into the fire bucket from which there was now an impressive firework display.

Most officers had a remarkably benevolent attitude and we were taken flying whenever possible. From Thorney Island some of us flew to Germany in a 4-engine Miles/Handley Page Marathon, and returned next morning in time for breakfast. From RAF Kinloss, in Scotland, we were taken flying in Avro Shackletons which had an amazing endurance, some 20 hours. Its only creature comfort was a small galley. It was cold and draughty, and it rattled and shook. Several incidents with unsecured hatches delayed our take-off and our night time attack on an 'enemy submarine' was meant to straddle it with our practice bombs. Judging by the comments of the Range Officer we had not only missed our target but nearly destroyed his bunker. He seemed to feel that with people like us in the sky there was a secure future in the Russian Navy although he could not say the same for our allies. Shortly after that, one of the crew sat down, but not for long, on the cooker. It took a few seconds for him to realise that it had been accidentally switched on by one of our cadets. The officer with a singed bottom promptly set about enriching but not improving the cadet's vocabulary. In fact, inquisitive cadets who pulled levers or pressed switches without asking were a menace. A group of us were taken flying from RAF North Weald in an ancient Anson. Bored with sitting in a seat and looking at the view from 2,000 feet one of our group wandered towards the door.

'What do you think this lever does?' he asked.

'Pull it and see what happens,' we chorused.

The door vanished in a rush of air that very nearly sucked him out and terrified all on board. Another cadet jettisoned the cockpit canopy of a Meteor T7 while flying at some 300 knots. In fact, we were later banned from flying in this type, not because of the canopy episode but because this mark of Meteor could not accommodate two ejector seats.

The first simulator we experienced was at RAF Bassingbourne where we lay prone and became bomb aimers. It proved surprisingly difficult but when we had mastered the calculations for wind and altitude corrections we then flew in that most elegant of British designs, the Canberra, an aircraft that was a decade ahead of its time. No bombs were dropped, however. For me the greatest treat of all was to fly in a single engine Chipmunk as we were allowed to handle the controls and feel the aircraft respond to our hand and feet movements – it was magic. The magic minutes in the air were worth all the travel time and standing in line to await my turn. I knew I wanted to fly myself. Shortly afterwards I was selected to join a small group to spend a week at RAF Halton where a team of dedicated instructors taught us to fly gliders.

Anyone who complains that there is too much time spent waiting around for flying obviously has not tried gliding. We spent hours tugging, heaving and preparing the machines for flight and recovering them afterwards. Nevertheless it was fun and more than amply repaid by the blissful moments of silent flight with just the moan of the wind and comments from our instructors to disturb the peacefulness. A week later we graduated with our A and B certificates. Our enthusiastic instructors seemed to share our pleasure and I still look forward to flying sailplanes again.

As we stood in line our logbooks were duly signed and stamped by the Commanding Officer. Holding his newly signed document aloft Jeffrey, one of our group, turned and smiled at the rest of us.

'Well, that was something to look back on,' he exclaimed.

Far from looking back, I was already looking forward. For me the next step was important – powered flight.

CHAPTER 4

# Panshanger

M Y INTEREST IN FLYING was tolerated, if not encouraged, by my parents and family. However, a friend of my parents, George, who had flown Mosquitoes in World War II became my confidant and adviser. It was George who told me about Panshanger aerodrome and George who promised to introduce me to one of the country's most experienced flying instructors. Furthermore, it was George who told me about a forthcoming flying display at Panshanger and George who persuaded my father to take me to it. I could hardly contain my excitement as I navigated my father's car through the winding roads of Hertfordshire.

Panshanger aerodrome was located off a winding country road not far from Cole Green in Hertfordshire. At first glance it was not impressive. It was a large green field almost adjacent to Welwyn Garden City, and a short distance from Hatfield. After the smart guard house, neatly arranged fire extinguishers and immaculate lawns of the RAF airfields, Panshanger seemed almost derelict. As we drove in I could not help but notice the weeds that flourished among the cracked pavement areas, a few military pattern Nissen huts with curved corrugated iron roofs that appeared to have seen better days and long grass everywhere. None of this mattered, of course: it was the aircraft that were important.

We parked in a muddy, bumpy section of the airfield and

stood in line to buy a programme. We were told that each
programme was numbered and that the winner of a lucky
draw would be taken for a short flight in a Tiger Moth. We
had struck lucky with the weather which was perfect with
just a few cumulus clouds in the blue sky. A few aircraft of
British manufacture stood pointing into the wind and we
wandered towards the barrier awaiting the commencement
of the display. The voice of the announcer echoed across the
field.

Even now, I still remember the Miles Messenger being put
through its paces. It was a small wooden four-seater
monoplane, low wing, with triple fins, large flaps and
unbelievable handling at slow speed. When flown against the
light breeze it hardly seemed to move, and yet was nimble
when speed was required. Another visitor was the Auster
Aiglet. The Auster was one of the few British light aircraft
still in production, and was to be found in many flying clubs.
This was a high wing monoplane of metal construction but
covered with canvas. The Aiglet was a recently produced
aerobatic version of the touring aircraft and it was to be
displayed by Auster's chief test pilot Ronald Porteus. His
6 ft. frame around which all Austers appeared to have been
built was later to be a source of embarrassment to me but he
certainly knew how to fly. The chief pilot himself was
present to display this latest version of the Auster family.
Somehow he inserted his large frame into the small aircraft
and we watched as the little silver high-winged monoplane
climbed at full power into the cloud-studded sky.

'We are in for a treat,' said the man next to me. I looked at
his blue RAF blazer with a squadron badge and his trim
moustache.

'He looks as though he should know what he is talking about,' I thought.

Still on full throttle the aircraft turned over our heads, the nose dropped into a shallow dive and it pulled into a vertical climb all in one seamless manoeuvre. The silver machine was continuing onto its back as if to loop when, suddenly, it spun around its long axis and continued with the recovery from a loop.

'What on earth was that?' I gasped.

'That's a Porteus Loop,' explained my new-found friend. 'It's a manoeuvre he designed. It's basically a loop with a complete roll built in at the top. For a few seconds you have to hold the stick in a spin position and it takes fine judgement. Watch carefully as he has several tricks up his sleeve.'

He was right. For the next minutes the crowd fell silent as the silver arrow traced intricate patterns against the cloudy backdrop. The engine noise waned and strengthened as this amazing aerial ballet continued without pause. For a brief moment the machine appeared to stop in midair then it began to slide downwards and sideways.

'Here comes a falling leaf,' my neighbour called.

This was a highly descriptive term for the descent of the Aiglet. We held our breath as there appeared no attempt at recovery until disaster was imminent. At the last instant a little burst of power was applied and the aircraft dropped over the boundary of the airfield to make a perfect three point landing. We all burst into spontaneous applause.

'Wait until he switches off his engine as he can't hear you,' announced a muffled voice from the loudspeaker. Nobody had thought of that.

The time was approaching for the lucky draw as I waited hoping for a chance to fly in the open cockpit biplane that was sitting tantalizingly on the grass a few yards from me. Much to my disappointment I did not win the lucky draw. It was won by a strangely dressed old woman. I would have willingly changed places with her as she showed no great enthusiasm to fly and had to be encouraged by well-wishers and by her pilot. Half pulled and half carried, the winner inched her way across the few yards of grass before she was hauled, complete with bulging handbag, into the rear cockpit of the Tiger Moth. The pilot climbed into the front, a mechanic swung the propeller by hand and the engine burst into life. As the chocks in front of the wheels were pulled away I felt pangs of jealousy but then realised all was not well in the rear cockpit. The passenger was waving her handbag over her head with one hand and banging the side of the cockpit with the other. With all the excitement of loading the passenger nobody had thought of stowing the luggage.

The pantomime behind at last attracted the pilot's attention. The engine slowed to tick over as the pilot climbed out of his cockpit, jumped down from the wing and approached his passenger. After some shouting and gesticulating the offending bag was passed over the edge of the cockpit hatch – then it all went wrong. Somehow the passenger's sleeve must have caught the throttle lever for with a sudden roar the engine went to full power. In vain the pilot battled against the slipstream as he tried to catch up with the aircraft that was accelerating away from him. Two other helpers sprinted for the tailplane but the Tiger outpaced them all. A shocked silence fell over the crowd as the pilotless aircraft, now with its tail up, swerved and lurched across the airfield. We imagined we heard the screams of the frightened passenger who was desperately waving.

'Stay still, don't worry, we're doing all we can,' came a hesitant voice echoing from the loudspeakers. By some miracle the Tiger Moth had taken off by itself but the crowd's concern for its passenger turned to more selfish thoughts as the machine skidded through 180 degrees and came back over the airfield boundary headed straight for us. Some screamed, one or two threw themselves flat, but most stood transfixed watching this imminent disaster approaching. The plane swayed from side to side and at the last minute the left wing dropped, I felt sure it actually brushed the grass, and the aircraft turned away and disappeared between two hangars. There was no sickening thud, no explosion, just another miracle as the Tiger emerged on the other side in a wobbling climbing turn. By now the fire engine was in full swing tearing around the field trying to estimate the point of the crash. It almost seemed as if the old lady was actually trying to land the aircraft but all she was achieving was a series of terrifying bounces. After four such leaps, the right wing dropped and the aircraft headed straight for the fire engine. The firemen leaped from their machine and flattened themselves on the ground, but in the nick of time the aircraft lifted over their prostrate bodies, missed the fire engine by a whisker and began a hesitant turn towards us.

'Take cover under the cars,' shouted one of the crowd, as people began backing away from the flight line. Just then the loudspeakers crackled into life.

'Relax everyone,' came a cheerful announcement. 'The

Tiger Moth is being flown by our Chief Flying Instructor,' laughed the commentator. 'We thought it might just get your attention!'

Not everyone was amused but I was staggered. The Chief Flying Instructor was Derek de Sarigny, the man that George had spoken about and my future instructor.

After the display was over George took us to meet the great man. Derek was wearing an old tweed jacket with leather patches on the elbows. He was of average build, slightly balding, and held a long cigarette holder between his teeth. He also sported a neat moustache. For a moment he ignored us as he appeared to be carrying out a detailed inspection of the Auster Aiglet that had been so brilliantly displayed. In my innocence I had not realised the strong competitive streak that runs through the veins of some display pilots. I was about to find out.

'I'm going to see how this aircraft handles,' he said pensively. 'Come with me by all means.' Derek turned towards George and stared hard. 'He's not going to be sick on me, is he?'

Both heads turned in my direction.

'Of course not,' I replied with as much confidence as I could muster. Derek showed me the cockpit, and seemed to spend a great deal of time ensuring that my safety harness was tight, painfully tight in fact. We taxied across the bumpy grass field. 'Harness and hatches secure,' Derek called out and opened the throttle.

Apart from the noise there was a series of ever increasing bumps and then we were airborne, climbing steeply away from the field. Beneath us the crowd was making its way home and a traffic jam was spreading outwards from the

aerodrome. Still the climb continued then the nose dropped
to level flight – but only briefly.

'Check for other aircraft!' he shouted as the left wing
dropped and we spun around the wing tip, then we were
diving. Some giant was squeezing me into the seat as we
climbed ever more steeply until I was lying on my back, then
the world went crazy. Sky, clouds and ground all seemed to
rotate but in no perceptible order. Shortly afterwards I was
clutching my seat for dear life as we hung on our straps
upside down.

'Your Dad's up there!' yelled Derek, pointing up through
the roof.

'Hold tight!' he cried as we climbed inverted and some
unseen force tried to pull me away from the seat. That was
the last clear recollection I had as the earth began to spin. I
tried to prevent myself being thrown through the roof of the
aircraft having lost all sense of orientation and balance. I was
sure that I would vomit but slowly became aware that the
rotation had stopped, although the strain on my harness
increased to what I imagined was breaking point and then we
rolled upright. This was my introduction to the inverted
spin, a masochistic exercise I was to hate for years to come.

'Time to go home,' called Derek.

'That was great,' I lied through gritted teeth, hoping that I
was not going to be sick.

We touched down with scarcely a bump and I manipulated
what I hoped was a confident smile as we taxied towards the
small waiting crowd. From what was said our display was
even more impressive when viewed from the ground and
surviving it had taken me across the first hurdle towards
flying lessons.

Derek de Sarigny was a man to take seriously and
commanded respect wherever he went. His father was
rumoured to have been a World War One fighter ace. Derek
was certainly steeped in knowledge and flying tradition. He
appeared to be expert on all aspects of aviation and held
strong views about most of them. Years of military and
civilian experience had left their mark while he seemed to
have a boundless thirst for new knowledge. Derek could
expound on his love for archaeology, his interest in medical
science, but when it came to flying he was in a league of his
own.

The Tiger Moth which formed the backbone of most
flying clubs could hardly have been a simpler aircraft. It had
no electrical system, no flaps and no brakes but listening
to Derek's explanations of the functions of every small
component was a revelation. A host of spare parts when
assembled in the shape of an aircraft behaved like a human
being. Each machine had individual characteristics and
behaviour patterns. Even starting the engine appeared to
have a special routine, taking particular care to ensure that
chocks were placed in front of the wheels as the aircraft had
no brakes. The first flight of the day involved lifting the
starboard engine cowl, priming the carburettor (more on
some machines than others) and ceremoniously tapping the
impulse magneto. Only then could you set about trying to
start the engine.

Hand swinging a propeller required care and skill. Horror
stories of fingers or thumbs being lost made sure that we
kept our thumbs adjacent to our fingers during this exercise.
It required team effort between pilot and the helper who
required implicit confidence that the magneto switches really

were off when the pilot said they were. The handler swinging the propeller was technically in charge of the starting operation. 'Switches off' meant that all the magneto switches were off. On the Tiger Moth the switches were just outside the open cockpit so that the switch position could be checked. An important lesson was the art of shifting body weight while propeller swinging so that if you slipped you were not decapitated by the propeller. Somehow just being with these aircraft was exciting and the smell of fuel, aircraft dope and cut grass was enough to make the heart beat faster.

Before each flight we had a very thorough briefing together with a question and answer period. This was just as well because it was extremely difficult to communicate while airborne. The instructor sat in the front cockpit so that the pupil could see hand signals. However, speech above the engine and wind noise was virtually impossible. Instead, an open speaking tube in front of the instructor led to the pupil's helmet, and a similar arrangement worked the other way round. Blowing down the tube certainly got attention, if somewhat unwelcome, but at least half of any conversation was lost. As a pupil you tended to use the voice level as a measure of progress. An increasing volume was a reliable measure of displeasure from the front.

The Tiger Moth was a delight to fly. We were taught to hold the control column between thumb and two fingers and it required coordination between hand and feet to fly well. While the central bracing wires could be used like a gun sight to maintain the nose level during turns, a blast of air on the side of your face informed you and your instructor that an incorrect amount of rudder had been applied.

When Derek called 'I have control,' I never knew what to

expect. It could either be a demonstration of what I should have been doing, or an exaggerated display of what Derek felt might happen if I continued with what I was actually doing.

'Do what I say – not what I do' appeared to be a maxim common in aviation.

Landings required considerable finesse. The aircraft was responsive to the slightest gust and any landing not directly into wind required a great deal of concentration and coordination. Although a joy to fly the Tiger Moth was no respecter of experience or age. We always thought it amusing to watch airline captains who wished to acquaint or re-acquaint themselves with the Tiger Moth. Any tendency to a condescending attitude quickly vanished after the first attempted landing as the aircraft bounced across the field like a demented kangaroo until the throttle was frantically opened and another attempt made – this time with more input from the instructor.

Our small group of three consisted of Paul, a serious and meticulous teenaged student, Harvey, with a far more relaxed approach to flying, and myself. We learnt that an older man in his thirties was to join us. Frank was quietly spoken and said he had never seen a Tiger Moth at close quarters and so Derek instructed me to show him the aircraft. Frank listened in rapt attention as I showed him every detail of the machine and watched as I moved the control column and the elevators and ailerons moved in the correct manner. Since he seemed so interested I even showed him the compass and explained how it was used. Frank seemed to pick things up quickly for such an elderly man. A week later I hid my head in shame. Frank was an ex World War II bomber pilot in the

RAF with a DFC! Somehow he had trained abroad and had not flown Tiger Moths hence the misunderstanding. Being a true gentleman my basic instruction lesson was never mentioned again – nor do I think he mentioned it to anyone else. Despite his experience, we were surprised how much of the course Frank was required to complete to obtain his civil licence. He was serious, quietly spoken and should have served as a role model for us youngsters. However, we knew better!

Derek set extraordinary standards. His pupils had to demonstrate stalls, spins and recovery procedures with an automatic reflex. Forced landing techniques became instinctive and this was to stand me in good stead later on. Circuits were flown in a precise military style pattern, the only variation being when Derek took over control. The Tiger Moth had slats on the leading edges of the upper wings that extended automatically as the aircraft approached the stall. The combination of the low wing loading and extended slats permitted the Tiger Moth to be flown amazingly slowly and no one could fly it more slowly than Derek.

After the completion of a landing run we might be faced with a long tedious snail paced taxi back to the Club House across the rollercoaster contours of the airfield. Instead, Derek would open the throttle, become airborne, and then throttle back so that the aircraft flew on the brink of a stall, slats extended, with its wheels brushing the top of the grass. As we neared the Club House the throttle would be closed and the aircraft would come to rest by its parking position. For deliberate stalls and aerobatic manoeuvres, the leading edge slats could be locked closed by operating a lever in the cockpit. One had to remember to unlock them afterwards.

Since there was no radio and no control tower, circuit procedures and a good look out were the means of avoiding collisions. It worked surprisingly well. After completing the landing run the rule was to clear the runway by turning left. Since the runway was a field it was quite safe to land close behind another aircraft provided that you landed on its right. One day a crop spraying Tiger Moth finished its landing run and turned right making a beeline for its hangar. Unfortunately, for the crop spraying pilot, Derek was the instructor in the machine behind.

'I have control,' called Derek as he opened the throttle, bounced the aircraft on the grass a few feet from the offending aircraft, and skimmed its top wing by a whisker. Before the pilot had recovered, Derek's Tiger Moth completed a low level turn and landed by the crop sprayer's hangar. The shaken pilot taxied to his base to find the Chief Flying Instructor, arms crossed, awaiting him. Derek's pupil slid down into his cockpit and pretended not to be there as the fracas started. Quite what was said no one ever knew but from that time on all pilots made sure they turned left after landing.

A week later I bounced on landing, recovered and finished my landing run with a red face. Derek climbed out of the front cockpit, but instead of criticism, he smiled.

'I was waiting for that. You are just about ready to go solo when we get some good weather.'

My first solo did not in fact take place under Derek's critical gaze for I had just won an RAF flying scholarship. The scholarship meant that I could learn to fly at a civilian establishment chosen by the RAF and that most of the course would be paid for. There was an understanding that when I was called up for my compulsory military service I would join the RAF but this did not appear to be a great drawback. I was told to report to the Surrey Flying Club that was to be found at Croydon Airport. Derek, who had now become a family friend, encouraged me to leave his care, at least for the time being.

CHAPTER 5

# Croydon Days

THE VERY NAME Croydon was evocative. Even those with the slightest knowledge of aviation would know of the important role of this airport in British Aviation. Compared with Panshanger it was vast, with a string of hangars, a terminal building and a hotel all parallel to the main road, Purley Way. On entering the main terminal to seek directions I was struck by an atmosphere of good days gone by. Although not dirty it seemed musty. A large control tower sat above the terminal. Many aircraft, like our own, carried no radio, and so the controller had to use light signals for the smaller aircraft and radio for the larger machines. The area in front of the terminal was covered in tarmac but the airfield was basically grass which came as a surprise. The first few metres of each runway were covered in tarmac, and we later discovered a wire mesh under the grass of the runway which prevented aircraft sinking into the mud but made a strange rumbling noise on take-off and landing. There was a pronounced slope down from south to north and this became highly significant when you attempted to taxi an aircraft downwind, downhill, with no brakes and no tail wheel. It was to be a source of considerable embarrassment later on.

On leaving the terminal I came to the hangars of Rollason Aircraft towards the south-east of the airport. This thriving

46

*Croydon Airport. The downward slope of the tarmac in front of the*
*buildings from left to right was the cause of several mishaps*
*(photography courtesy of Tom Samson, The Croydon Airport Society).*

concern serviced and even built aircraft. My new home, the
Surrey Flying Club, was just a little further along the road.
The Surrey Flying Club was a wood framed building that
looked rather flimsy. The first impression on entering was
that of stale beer but there was an immediate aura of
camaraderie and friendship. A large bar dominated the
building. It was here that I met my instructor and my fellow
cadets on the course. After the usual introductions the cadets
were divided into groups and assigned instructors. My
instructor was Tony Richmond. Tony had a winning smile
and a warm manner. I took an immediate liking to him.
Peter, one of the cadets, whispered that Tony had been a test
pilot for Blackburn aircraft with a great deal of wartime and
post-war experience on high performance machines.

Tony examined my logbook and asked a few technical questions about the Tiger Moth. Thanks to Derek's training I felt immediately at ease in the cockpit. We received our green light and took off. The runway was much smoother than that at Panshanger; I automatically called out my check lists and flew around the circuit without problem. There were so many landmarks that the circuit was easily defined. After several circuits we taxied back to the Club House.

'Well you seem to know what you're doing,' said Tony. 'I'd like you to take the Chief Flying Instructor around the circuit. I'll take you over to meet him.'

Tiny Marshall was huge. He wandered over to me, goggles in hand.

'Take me round the circuit,' he commanded in a gruff manner.

Tiny's huge frame in the front cockpit obliterated what little direct forward vision there was. He planted his goggles on his forehead, checked that we had a green light and off we went.

There was absolute silence from the front until the third landing. He signalled for me to taxi back to the beginning of the runway and then climbed out of his cockpit. As he came alongside me he shouted above the engine noise.

'Think you can manage a circuit on your own?'

'Yes, Sir!' I shouted back.

'Bugger off then,' he said, 'Don't forget to pick me up after landing.'

Relieved of Tiny's weight the little biplane shot up into the clear air. It was only when I levelled out that I became aware of the empty cockpit ahead. All pilots on their first solos must have savoured this unique excitement. The slight turbulence, the nearby cooling towers and the green light from the control tower were all engraved on my memory. In a few moments the circuit was completed and the landing good. I was so excited I nearly forgot Tiny waiting by the edge of the runway. Of course, there were drinks all round in the Club House, and since I had gone solo on my first day with the Club, it was going to leave me with free time at the end of the course filling in the requisite number of hours. This free time was to get me into trouble later on. Meanwhile there was plenty of time to enjoy cadet life and to make new friends. Of course there was friendly rivalry between us but my rapid start had placed me well ahead of all the others. Once I had demonstrated that I could fly around the circuit in most weather conditions, we put into practice the navigation lessons we had learnt.

Flying away from the airfield was one thing, finding it again was not always so straightforward. At Croydon we were lucky as the cooling towers at Coulsdon could be seen from miles away and these towers were virtually on the circuit. The eastern border of the airfield was marked by the main road, Purley Way, and there was a swimming pool to assist in planning the arrival in the circuit. When the weather was not clear we had a special route to follow known as a Free Lane. This route took us south down a valley towards a railway station at Godstone with clearly visible gas holders. Once clear of the range of hills, the North Downs, the pilot could turn east or west and there were railway lines to follow. It all seemed so simple: it was amazing the speed at which overconfidence built – then evaporated.

Meanwhile, back at our base at Croydon Airport life was not so smooth. Bill, one of my cadet friends, had to taxi a

Tiger Moth across the tarmac in front of the terminal. He
had forgotten the need to take a helper who could hold a
wing tip to help him turn or grab the tail plane to help him
stop. Instead, Bill arrived on the tarmac at a healthy speed
oblivious of the wind behind him and the downward slope
ahead of him. Too late he realised that he could not stop and
lacked the skill to turn. Directly in his path lay a Dakota into
which a group of passengers had just embarked. Of course,
Bill could have cut the engine. He could even have leapt out
and grabbed the tail but he did nothing. At the last moment
the Captain of the Dakota realised that the Tiger Moth was
on a collision course. His face could be seen at the storm
window. The mechanics who had just closed the cabin door
were waving frantically but Bill stared ahead, transfixed by
the rapidly approaching left wing-tip of the Dakota. With a
horrible tearing noise his propeller took its first bite of the
canvas covered aileron and continued to eat its way along the
control surface. I cannot recall who it was that cut the
magneto switches and restored peace. An engineer and flight
attendant led the passengers into the terminal followed by a
red-faced captain with a neat moustache. Fortunately for Bill,
the captain was already hoarse from shouting. He did
however manage to croak, 'You stupid, ignorant bastard,
you're not only unfit to fly a plane, I'm going to see to it that
you never even fly a paper dart!'

He was wrong. Bill later became a senior training captain
in British Airways.

Malcolm, one of our group, was very amused at Bill's
discomfort and never failed to tease him.

'Would you like me to walk in front of your bicycle?' he
enquired unkindly.

The teasing came to an abrupt halt the following week when Malcolm found himself headed downhill straight towards a hangar wall. Fortunately he switched off the magnetos before the collision so that it was only pride that was damaged. It was an effective lesson to us all.

Our bar was visited by pilot members of the Club and also by the Tiger Club, an elite band of experienced pilots whose aircraft were maintained by Rollason's next door. Almost without exception the group were friendly, helpful, and a fund of knowledge. Occasionally we were even allowed to fly in their immaculately prepared machines. Giles was the exception. He was not just aloof but downright arrogant. I was not present to witness the humbling of Giles but I heard a great deal about it. Evidently Giles was taking a farmer friend for his first flight. Instead of briefing his passenger and removing the control column from the front cockpit Giles had spent ten minutes regaling his passenger, and nearby cadets, with tales of his exploits in the air.

One of the cadets swung the propeller and Giles taxied out. The first part of the take-off run appeared normal until the passenger became aware of a rod that was playing against his inner thighs. Without any further thought he pushed it smartly away. The Tiger Moth pitched smartly onto its nose and the engine stopped mid beat, the propeller splintered and slowly, as in slow motion, the aircraft tumbled onto its back. There was a stunned silence then pandemonium as the emergency services and onlookers ran to the crash scene. Any worries about occupants vanished as they came closer. Giles had released his harness and fallen on to his head but with no serious effects. He was sitting on the grass rubbing his head as the helpers rushed up.

'Get me out of the goddamned contraption,' yelled the irate passenger still upside down in the front cockpit.

'Don't release your harness,' shouted the first helper. 'You'll fall on your head.'

The furious passenger was extracted from the cockpit; he brushed himself down and glared at poor Giles who was still sitting head in his hands.

'If that's what you call flying, it's only for fools!' he grunted, and stalked off across the aerodrome. The Tiger Moth was repaired surprisingly quickly and Giles became friendly and pleasant company.

At the rather sedate cruising speed of 80-90 m.p.h. the effect of a 20 m.p.h. wind on the nose or the beam, or on the tail became highly significant. We all became adept at using the Dalton computer to assist in flight planning and calculating our ground speed and drift. Our instructors checked our calculations as it was all too easy to apply drift the wrong way and if you did get lost there was no radio to ask for help. One lesson was to recognize the importance of the watch as a navigational instrument. After all, if you duly recorded the time at which you passed a confirmed landmark and then flew a steady heading at a known speed for a known time you simply had to be within a fairly small prescribed area, at least that is the story they told us. In fact inexperienced pilots when uncertain of their position often turned from one side to another or clutched at straws in the form of roads or railway lines and failed to check their compass against the feature they were following. Then they were really lost.

Railways were in plentiful supply in south-east England and it was a question of making sure you were following the right one. The best line has guided many generations of British aviators. It runs east-west, straight as an arrow, from Ashford in Kent, not far from the port of Folkestone, to Tonbridge. To find Croydon, you flew along this straight line to Godstone and then turned north up the valley. We began to gain confidence but we also worked out our own methods of finding our way around when the weather was not so good.

If uncertain of our position, we set aside much of what we had learnt and simply flew until we found a railway line. The Tiger Moth was then flown at low level until it came to a station and the pilot would read the name on the platform. If the name could not be found on the map, he followed the line until a larger town appeared. The lower the cloud the lower he flew. The fact that such manoeuvres were both dangerous and illegal may have crossed our minds but not for long. Our instructors would have been horrified had they known of these antics. Hills, masts, buildings and even trees were often enveloped in cloud and it is almost a miracle that no one actually hit anything solid. Scud running, as it is called in the United States, continues to claim the lives of novice and experienced pilots. Faced with an unexpected deterioration in weather we should have returned to base, diverted to another airfield or, if really trapped, considered a forced landing. As it transpired we were inexperienced, overconfident, and lucky. We were also saved by the amazing manoeuvrability, forgiving nature and impeccable low speed handling of the Tiger Moth.

The best excuse we were given for low flying was an instruction to practise forced landings. These were constantly undertaken as our instructors drummed into us the

unreliability of aero engines. We found out that the little
Tiger Moth could be flown around trees, could skim hedges,
or even land on a football field. I was the first unlucky pilot
to be challenged with a complaint. My detail had been to
practise forced landings on Redhill aerodrome that was
temporarily closed. I did this with gusto. Unfortunately, one
of the neighbours was not only a pilot who knew where the
aircraft was based but telephoned the Chief Flying Instructor
with a graphic description of the way the aircraft was being
flown. For good measure he even suggested that his H shape
television aerial had been damaged, and now resembled an
inverted U. In fact I had been caught out by lowering cloud
and was only just able to sneak up the valley from Godstone
back to Croydon. I wondered why the CFI inspected my
aircraft so carefully after the flight but there was no sign of
any damage or pieces of television aerial. Nevertheless, I
received a thoroughly deserved admonition about selfish
behaviour, the hazards of low flying, and a reminder about
the law. Everything he said was correct, but I could not help
noticing a twinkle in his eyes. From then on we were all
more considerate. It also dawned upon us that if we were
flying low enough to read the signs on a railway station,
people on the railway station could just as easily read our
registration numbers. Railway lines sometimes went into
tunnels and this would come as a most unpleasant surprise
in conditions of poor visibility!

Part of the licence requirements included a cross-country
flight with two intermediate landings. This triangular route
with landings at Lympne and Shoreham, was not particularly
challenging as landmarks abounded. The first route was
flown with Tiny Marshall on board, the second time I flew

solo. There was never any shortage of helpers to swing propellers and it went smoothly. This exercise was normally flown at the end of the course but my rapid progress had left me with this hurdle behind me with many hours of flying still required to fulfil the flying time required for the licence. The Club therefore devised a series of navigation exercises for me to undertake and that is where the problems began.

CHAPTER 6

# Spreading the Wings

IT WAS NOT LONG before I could happily fly myself from
Croydon down to the South Coast, identify a landmark
and return on schedule. My navigational skills and
confidence increased daily and I began to look for new
adventures. All flights were strictly below cloud as we had no
instrument flying training and precious few instruments. I
was always tempted by the holes between the clouds of a
broken layer as the clear blue sky was beckoning beyond.
Like Oscar Wilde I could resist everything apart from
temptation. I yielded. I opened the throttle and slowly
climbed up between the puffs of cumulus. Above lay a
beautiful world of blinding sunshine, brilliant hues, silent
towering mountains and majestic snowy white cliffs. This
was not the picture book view sideways out of the small
window of an airliner. My little biplane was part of this awe-
inspiring view. Around the aircraft was a billowing white
mass. As I gingerly approached it there was a gentle 'whump'
as an air current struck the wings. I could pierce the side of
the cloud with a wing, and reach out of the cockpit and
touch the damp air of which the clouds were composed.

As I climbed higher I noticed the shadow of the biplane
on the cloud faithfully following every move; occasionally
the shadow was surrounded by a rainbow coloured halo.
Before long I was turning, diving and climbing in my secret

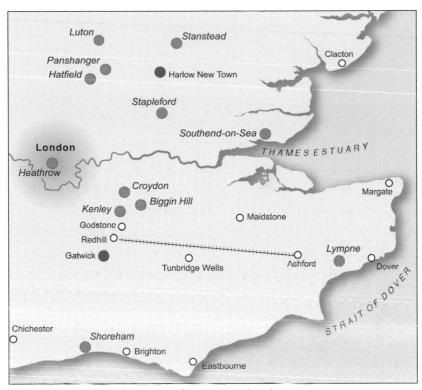

*South-east England.*

world of the clouds with all the enthusiasm of a kitten playing with a new ball of wool. Sometimes I imagined I was exploring the Arctic, or climbing in the Alps – I was completely alone. I only wished I could tell someone about it. Then came the descent through another hole, pin-pointing my position and flying back to Croydon with wide innocent eyes as if nothing untoward had occurred. Provided that I arrived back on schedule it looked as though I could complete my hours in this way. I was wrong. Aerobatics were definitely not part of the course. Naturally we would all do tight turns, enter spins and recover from them, but anything beyond these manoeuvres was not to be considered. Yet I longed to loop. After all, I reasoned, if some of the pioneers had managed it in their primitive machines with only a lap strap, why shouldn't I? It appeared that provided I kept the aircraft straight and gained enough speed, all I had to do was to apply enough back pressure to the control column and pull the machine over the top. I decided to make the attempt.

On my next navigational detail the weather was perfect. I needed a good landmark to keep track of my position and was pleased how clearly I could see the enormous man-made scar on the landscape that was the building of the new airport at Gatwick. To be on the safe side I thought I'd give myself plenty of altitude and climbed higher than I had ever climbed before. The temperature dropped quite markedly as I passed 5,000 ft. and I became aware that the aircraft was climbing less readily. At 8,000 ft. I levelled off.

The ground looked a long way off but Gatwick was easily spotted. As I made a few tight turns to make sure I was alone, and to gain confidence, I became aware that the aircraft was not quite so responsive to the controls and that the airspeed was lower than I expected. On full throttle I lowered the nose until the wind was whistling through the rigging wires and hauled back on the stick. The 'G' force compressed me into the seat and then the aircraft shuddered. Much to my amazement the aircraft spun off the top of the loop. Automatically I recovered realising that I had even forgotten to close the slats. I had pulled so hard I had stalled the poor machine. I realised this as I pulled out of the screaming dive, determined to try again. There was more to a loop than pulling the stick back. Looking back at Gatwick

I also realised I had changed my heading by more than 50 degrees – hardly surprising in view of the spin.

For my second attempt I added 10 m.p.h. to the diving speed and eased the stick back gently. This time I ran out of airspeed, spinning in the process. For an awful second I thought the spin might be inverted but I recovered without problem. For my third attempt I dived even faster and pulled the stick back slowly but firmly. A giant force squeezed me into the seat, and I felt that I was no longer flat on my back. Looking up I saw the blue sky give way to brown horizon and realised I was upside down. The next sensations happened almost simultaneously. I was no longer being held in the seat, and momentarily thought I was falling away from it, the engine coughed and died, and with a horrible shudder the nose dropped smartly as the ill treated aircraft stalled and tumbled downwards. The engine recovered at full throttle at about the time I realised the ground was dead ahead and I was diving vertically. By the time I had throttled back and regained a level altitude I had lost more than 2,000 ft. Thanks to the forgiving nature of the Tiger Moth I survived my adventure, but I had actually gone over the top and felt elated. The trouble was that no one else would ever know! Keeping Gatwick in sight I descended to the warmer and more familiar altitude of 2,000 ft. and then set course for Croydon.

There I made one of the neatest and shortest landings of my career so far and gleefully taxied back to the Club House. Climbing from the aircraft I was surprised to see the entire flying staff outside the Club House: surely my landing had not been that special? Two senior instructors, Tiny Marshall and Peter Chinn, were standing with Tony Richmond, and

behind them the cadets. As I approached it was obvious that
no one was smiling. I reassured myself that it was quite
impossible that anybody could have seen me at that height.
Closer still I could see that all the cadets were looking quiet
and subdued. Peter Chinn removed his pipe from between
his teeth and broke the silence.

'Cadet Preiskel, did you enjoy your aerobatics? Before you
say anything you are to telephone the Senior Air Traffic
Officer at West Drayton immediately; he is awaiting your
call.'

None of my friends looked at me as I made my way to the
Club House.

'How on earth did anyone know about my adventure, let
alone an Air Traffic Controller?' I was puzzled and worried
as I picked up the telephone and I began to think of all the
possible repercussions. My heart sank somewhere near my
knees.

The Senior Air Traffic Officer was cold, business-like, and
spoke with a clipped voice, 'Were you the pilot of an aircraft
operating in the Gatwick area at about 8,000 ft. around 12.00
hours?'

'Yes, Sir,' I replied timorously.

'Please spell your surname, and give me your licence
number.' I slowly spelt my name and then added, 'Sir, I
don't actually have a licence, only a student licence.'

'Would you mind explaining what you were doing at
8,000 ft. above Gatwick,' the steely voice enquired.

'Well, Sir, I was practising some manoeuvres,' I explained.

'And you had to choose the centre of one of the busiest
air lanes in Europe for this exercise. Do you know that
the Captain of a Viscount reported a biplane out of control

and that we have had to close this sector for the last half hour?'

'I'm terribly sorry, Sir, I had no idea about the airway. We normally operate at 2,000 ft. and I just needed some extra altitude for safety,' I replied truthfully.

'Not only did we have to reroute our inbound aircraft, we had trouble understanding your radar traces. Would you kindly explain your actions?'

There seemed nothing else to do other than to make a clean breast of the whole episode. Immediately, I detected a softening of his voice.

'I hope you understand the trouble you've caused and how irresponsible you have been. Fortunately, for you the Captain of the Viscount does not wish to file a complaint or air-miss as he was not close to you. Kindly pass the telephone to your Chief Flying Instructor.'

Peter Chinn took the phone and made me sit in a small room while my fate was decided. It seemed that at the very least I would be grounded for a period, I might have even thrown away my entire Flying Scholarship. My friends were obviously aware that I had committed a serious mis-demeanour but no one came near the little room. I even wondered about my forays above the clouds, but they had been much further south.

I waited in misery in Peter Chinn's office. I noted a damp patch on the wall, a faint musty smell and the much stronger aroma of stale tobacco, trying to put aside the thought that this marked the inevitable finish of my flying career before it had even started. After an eternity footsteps approached and I looked up, trying to disguise the inner turmoil of my thoughts. It was not Peter Chinn but a steely-faced Tony

Richmond who entered. Without a word he spun round, closed the door with the latch depressed, released the handle and shook the door gently to make sure it was properly shut. Slowly he turned around to face me. He was grinning!

'Did you actually get it over the top?' he enquired.

I nodded.

'Well you're a bloody fool not to have asked me for help. First of all you could have broken your stupid neck, secondly you're amazingly lucky that the CAA are not taking any action and thirdly, if you really want to do aerobatics, I'll teach you – but you mustn't tell anybody!'

I shook my head in disbelief.

'Do you realise the hazards of a tailslide?'

'Er, no.'

'Well if you get yourself in a vertical position, run out of airspeed, and the aircraft slides backwards, the airflow is reversed over the control surfaces. Unless you centre the control column and hold it firmly, the control surfaces will be forced to full deflection and then possibly be damaged or torn off by the airflow. You must keep your feet firmly planted on the rudder pedals to maintain a central position. The rudder is particularly vulnerable and without one you bail out. Then you're going to look pretty stupid without a parachute.'

I thought of my first attempt at a loop, but said nothing.

'In any case, I'm not going to fly with you for a while. You have to convince Tiny Marshall that you are still safe to fly an aircraft.'

I was not quite sure how I was going to manage my next encounter with Tiny. Tiny was a man of few words but spoke his mind, all too clearly at times. It was rumoured that he could let out a string of expletives for some fifteen minutes without repeating himself. After my exploits the day before, I trembled at the greeting I might receive.

'Fly me on a direct track to Lympne. Advise me when you have 10 miles to run to Ashford, identify Ashford and maintain 2,000 ft.,' he growled. 'I'll swing the prop.'

This did not seem too challenging and not a word came down the speaking tube as I taxied out, received my green light and took off.

The silence from the front was eerie as we cruised at 2,000 ft. Ahead of me the huge bulk of Tiny blotted out my forward view and I was fascinated by his goggles that were placed on his forehead, never over his eyes. Since his head must have been well above the windscreen I could not imagine how he could see with the full blast of the slipstream in his eyes. I became aware of a noise from the speaking tube.

'Climb to 3,500 ft. and level off,' he ordered.

We climbed to the new altitude and continued our leisurely cruise across the Kent countryside. I returned and started to admire the hills of the North Downs, the small woods, pretty farms...

'Check your harness,' rasped down the speaking tube.

'Harness secure,' I replied, rather puzzled.

'I have control,' Tiny called.

To my amazement he opened the throttle to maximum power, lowered the nose and allowed the speed to build up alarmingly. Then the nose came up smooth, steadily but firmly as I became forced down onto my seat cushion. I next remembered the control column hitting my right thigh as the horizon rotated. The next sensation was that of falling

out of the cockpit as I clutched my seat in terror. I imagined
the straps yielded less than an inch as we were upside down
but it felt as though I was falling out. Dirt from the cockpit
floated past me, the engine cut and I became aware of Tiny's
goggles floating above or rather below his head. Slowly the
horizon continued to rotate until we were upright again.
Tiny then repeated the manoeuvre rolling to the left, still
that awful sensation of falling out, Tiny's goggles floating
and then back to normal. I was later to find that the slow roll
required a great deal of hand and foot coordination in a Tiger
Moth and was one of Tiny's specialities. However, my
immediate concern was that the nose had dropped again but
this time we continued climbing without any rolling. The
horizon appeared upside down and then we were diving.
It was so smooth and apparently effortless and bore no
resemblance to my attempt at a loop. The airspeed was the
highest I had seen around 135 m.p.h. when Tiny pulled up
into what I assumed would be another loop. Just as the
horizon came into view he began to roll. Once again the
falling sensation and floating goggles then normality
returned. A voice was coming down the speaking tubes.

'That was two slow rolls, a loop, and a roll off the top.
Take me back to Croydon,' he rasped.

We flew back and landed in silence. As I climbed down for
my debriefing Tiny looked down on me.

'Was that interesting?' he said.

'Very much so,' I replied, looking into his eyes. There
were oil marks on his face and I wondered how he coped
with oil in his eyes.

'Well, bugger off then,' came the reply, but he was smiling.

As I came to know him I was to appreciate that Tiny was

one of the kindest and good natured people it was my privilege to have met. The gruff exterior was a camouflage.

My next few navigational exercises were flown strictly according to plan then I was handed back to Tony Richmond.

'Today's detail includes an introduction to the loop and a demonstration of the slow roll. Do you understand what is involved in both?' he asked.

'I've got two main fears,' I confessed. 'The first is falling out of the aircraft and the second is getting into an inverted spin.'

Tony smiled, 'It's true that in the RAF we used parachutes, and banned inverted spins, but I haven't yet met anyone who has fallen out of an aircraft. If you hold the stick back, the aircraft will spin normally even if you are inverted when you get into a spin – relax.'

This was not altogether reassuring as we set off southwards.

'We're not going to start any manoeuvres below 4,000 ft.,' yelled Tony as we did our precautionary turn to look for other aircraft, locked the slats and checked our harnesses.

'We need about 120 m.p.h. entry speed,' came his voice. 'If you pull back too sharply the aircraft will mush – you've increased the angle of attack too much and you'll never get around. If you are too gentle you'll run out of airspeed. Let's align ourselves with a landmark to keep straight and remember to close the throttle in the descent.'

Tony flew an effortless loop and then my own rather more ragged effort also succeeded. By the end of the lesson I could loop, not particularly elegantly, but I could definitely loop.

'We'll leave slow rolls for another time,' called Tony, 'Let's

go home. During your next cross country you must give me
your word not to attempt solo aerobatics,' Tony said in a
remarkably serious voice.

'I promise,' came the sincere reply.

'Your navigation is good,' Tony told me. 'But don't get
over confident. Always keep an eye on the time. A few years
ago I was testing the Blackburn Firebrand, one of the fastest
piston engine aircraft of its time. I was flying north over the
sea just off the East Coast so you can imagine my shock at
seeing the coastline on my *right*. I knew the aircraft was fast
but to cross the North Sea by mistake seemed impossible. It
took me a few minutes to realise I was over the Wash, that is
a large bay, and that is why I could see land on my right.
Even the most experienced of us become uncertain of our
position – be prepared.'

Tony took me for one of my last lessons before the Royal
Aero Club Test for my pilot's licence.

'The most common mistake during a slow roll is failure to
keep the nose up while inverted. You need a surprisingly
high angle of attack. Most novices hang on to the control
column for dear life with the result that the nose comes
down and they are diving vertically before they know what's
hit them. Remember the engine cuts.'

My first attempt at a slow roll was the classical novice's
attempt with a near vertical descent from the inverted. Tony
rescued the situation. The second roll was not too bad.

'Inverted flying, and understanding inverted manoeuvres
is difficult,' came Tony's reassuring voice down the tubes.
'You did pretty well, let's go back to base.'

The RAC flight test posed no particular problem and it
began to dawn upon me that I was about to obtain my

licence. This was thrilling. Unfortunately it also meant the end of the course. It was with great sadness that I said goodbye to Tony, Peter and Tiny. No one could have asked for better and more understanding teachers dedicated to their pupils. I promised them, and myself that I would return. Meanwhile I was to return to the care of Derek de Sarigny at Panshanger.

# CHAPTER 7

# Return to Panshanger

I RETURNED TO A warm welcome at Panshanger but the aerodrome looked different. It seemed small, some of the hangars appeared to be in disrepair, weeds grew between gaps in the concrete and the Club House seemed rather basic. My friends were still there, and that was what really mattered. Furthermore, Derek approved of the training I had received at Croydon and Derek's approval of other instructors was a rare accolade. Planning flights was a team effort and we all had to manipulate aircraft in and out of hangars, refuel them, and of course to swing propellers.

My first flight as Captain being checked out by Derek produced a few surprises. Panshanger was one grass field among the many of the rolling Hertfordshire countryside. It was hard to find. I had become used to Croydon with the large buildings, its control tower, the Coulsdon cooling towers, the swimming pool off Purley Way, and a host of other visual clues.

'Can you see the field?' Derek called down the tube.

'It must be in our 12 o'clock,' I called back.

'It was about a minute ago, you've just flown over it!' came the reply. 'If you look at the tarmac runway of Hatfield you'll see that it more or less points at Panshanger.'

I flew some circuits to Derek's satisfaction although I had forgotten about the bumpy grass runway.

'OK, fly me to the north towards Stevenage, climb to 4,000 ft. and don't cross any railway lines.'

As we levelled off Derek pointed out the two railway lines that converged at Stevenage and a line that joined them to the south, effectively making a triangle.

'Make a 180 degree tight turn to the right followed by a 180 degree turn to the left, roll out on a northerly heading,' came the next instruction.

I carried this out.

'That's fine; now I want to see a spin to the left and recover after three turns.'

None of these exercises worried me in the slightest.

'Fine,' said Derek. 'Can you manage a loop?'

Thanks to Tony I lined the aircraft on a road and produced my best loop to date.

'Let's go back home,' came the next instruction.

'Well,' said Derek, as we climbed out of the aircraft, 'you're safe to carry passengers in the Club aircraft. Don't even think of aerobatics on your own until we've spent time together. You have a great deal to learn.'

Carrying passengers was a thrill and there was never a shortage of volunteers among my student friends. The main problem was the weather as we had to wait for clear days. Even when one could fly, we found ourselves having to wear a great thickness of clothes for protection. My flying from Croydon took place in July and August. It was now November and the icy wind that whistled around the hangars was enough to freeze even the most hardened enthusiast. This paled into insignificance compared with sitting in an open cockpit when the slipstream felt like needles rather than a blast of freezing air.

*Tiger Moth over Essex.*

Nothing, however, was going to put us off our flying and nothing did.

I was tremendously excited to learn that Tony Richmond was coming to Panshanger. He was to demonstrate a new tourer to the flying club. This new aircraft was in fact a Tiger Moth converted to carry four people in a cramped cabin. The undercarriage had been strengthened and the separation between the wheels increased. The conversion was called the Jackaroo. In order to cope with the additional weight a propeller with a fine pitch was fitted. This helped with take-off and climb but reduced still further the sedate cruising speed of the Tiger Moth. It was rather like driving a car in second gear on the main road.

The day for the demonstration was awful with poor visibility. There was no flying at Panshanger that day and I could not imagine how Tony could possibly find it after a half hour journey from Thruxton. I need not have worried. Precisely on schedule a Gipsy Major engine was heard and the Jackaroo appeared out of the murk and touched down right in front of the Club House hardly using any runway. The meeting between Tony and Derek did not go well. They were polite and there was mutual respect but I had not foreseen the element of competition.

Derek as CFI took the Jackaroo around the circuit and made an even shorter landing than Tony. Tony as demonstrator took two club members around the circuit and landed shorter still. Eventually one of them went through the hedge, fortunately without any damage although that landing really was short. Tony disappeared into the gloom along with my hopes of bringing my heroes together.

With each flight Hertfordshire countryside became more familiar but the weather became colder. One of my earliest victims was a friend and classmate. Laurence was destined to become a distinguished future Sub-Dean of Guy's Hospital. He was always full of enthusiasm and happiness although his parents were of a more nervous disposition.

'We'd better not tell them,' said Laurence, and I agreed. It seemed sensible not to worry his parents as they were even concerned about their son travelling in my three-wheeled car.

I briefed Laurence thoroughly. Derek approved the flight.

'Stay within the railway triangle,' he reminded me as he swung the propeller and off we went. Ahead of me Laurence was sitting bolt upright in the front cockpit. Above lay a broken layer of cumulus.

'Are you enjoying the flight?' I enquired.

'I'm fine,' came the reply.

Anxious to impress my friend with my new skills I told him: 'Wait till you've seen this,' and climbed towards a break in the clouds. Upwards we climbed until that magic moment when we could bathe in the sunlight reflecting off the brilliant cloud tops. We squinted at the myriad reflections of the tiny ice crystals and the rainbow coloured shapes.

'Isn't that fantastic,' I called through the tubes. 'Look at this stunning cloudscape from horizon to horizon, it's like our own secret magic world.'

Laurence seemed strangely unimpressed and continued to stare ahead, I noticed him reaching for the speaking tube.

'How are we going to get down?' he asked.

I was about to tell him not to be so stupid when I realised he was right. We were looking down on a *solid* cloudscape, not a hole in sight. This really did pose a problem so I turned onto a southerly heading as I knew the magnetic compass was more sensitive in this direction. This would at least give me a sporting chance of holding the aircraft straight, watching the slip and turn and hoping that we broke out beneath the cloud before I lost control. All of a sudden the clouds lost their beauty and became menacing as we sank downwards towards them. Suddenly a small opening appeared; actually it was very small indeed, but I could see a dark patch of ground down below. One thing I could do was to turn the little biplane on its wing tip and our descent must have resembled a vertical corkscrew. In retrospect I should have advised Laurence of my intentions but there really had not been enough time. We gyrated earthwards with the wind screaming its protest.

Strange noises were coming down the speaking tube.

These ceased as I pulled out of the dive and the G-forces compressed Laurence into his seat.

'That was fun,' I called cheerily. 'Are you enjoying it?'

'Ughh,' came the unconvincing reply.

A strange sinking sensation came from my stomach as I looked for landmarks. According to my estimate we should have been over Epping Forest, but all I could see was a town. Nothing I saw related to the features on my map. My overconfidence evaporated like a pricked balloon. Noises were coming down the tube. Laurence's normal firm and resonant voice seemed surprisingly broken.

'I want to land,' he croaked.

'We just need to recheck our position,' I called with as much confidence as I could muster. I spotted the railway line and the station at about the same moment. 'We are going to fly fairly low along the railway line and when we go through the station I want you to read the name of it,' I called, as if this was everyday navigational practice. After all this was his first flight and maybe he would believe this was normal procedure. Laurence seemed strangely restless as we skimmed above the railway tracks. Maybe as a railway passenger he hadn't seen too many aircraft fly through railway stations while he had been standing on the platform. I was certain that the waiting passengers on the station we flew through were surprised, but I read the name on the platform, *Harlow*.

For a horrible moment I thought Laurence might use the speaking tube as a sick bag but all that transpired was a message:

'OK?'

'Fine,' I lied as I could not find Harlow on my map. It was

no use, we were lost but I spied a bus just out of the town proceeding down a straight road. I could see no trees, high tension cables or telegraph poles. I throttled back and headed down the road that was into wind.

'Read the destination board on the bus,' I called to Laurence as we followed it a few feet above the tarmac. I could make out white faces but suddenly realised the back of the bus was hurtling towards us. The driver must have braked. We had enough airspeed to climb and avoid it but the excitement was proving too much for Laurence.

With an apologetic smile, Laurence half turned and was promptly sick – straight into my face. The effect was devastating. My windscreen and goggles were covered. Instinctively I climbed to a safe height before realising that the problem was far worse than the mess and stench. Some of the vomit was in my eyes and they were already stinging. I suddenly realised I might lose my vision and an immediate forced landing was necessary. There was a deathly silence from the front when I explained we were to make a precautionary landing. I selected a reasonably sized field and began my descent but as I came closer my passenger appeared to go mad. In front of me, Laurence was gesticulating wildly with his left arm but seemed to have his mouth covered with his right hand, giving the appearance of a warlike Indian from a silent Wild West film. I continued my approach but Laurence's distress became greater still.

'What's the problem?' I shouted down the tube.

At last, following his outstretched hand, I was able to see the cause of his alarm. Laurence had a grandstand view of a thin wire fence stretched across our proposed landing site that would have brought our arrival to an abrupt halt. I opened the throttle and we climbed away.

'Why on earth didn't he tell me about it,' I puzzled.

The answer came quickly. My windscreen and goggles received a second coating and I realised that my unfortunate passenger had been quite unable to shout any warning down the speaking tube. It was becoming increasingly urgent that we landed quickly while I still had some vision remaining. Laurence now appeared relaxed – too relaxed in fact, because he was slumped forward in the cockpit and I now had to come to terms with the possibility that he was not enjoying his first flight.

Then I remembered the playing field I had seen minutes earlier. It looked long enough. I side-slipped around a block of flats and landed diagonally across a rugby pitch. We had landed in a school playing field during break and we were mobbed by schoolchildren, masters, and a few members of the public who had witnessed our arrival.

Laurence's appearance produced a sympathetic reaction from most of the onlookers. The children were more interested in the aircraft.

'Nearly took me bleeding 'ead orf,' confided one of the youngsters.

'Can I sit in the cockpit, mister?' asked another.

'Did you fly in the war?' enquired an earnest child.

'Take us for a ride, mister,' begged another.

We were saved by the masters who recovered their charges and made them stand at a respectable distance. Another master helped me pin-point our position on the map. Harlow New Town, as it was called, had been built since my map was printed: no wonder I couldn't find it. Around us

*The* Harlow Citizen. *Plane comes down in school field.*

chaos reigned. Neighbours were rushing onto the field and then the police arrived. Since everyone had seen Laurence climb out of the front cockpit he was assumed to be the pilot. Laurence was in no state to deny it or anything else for that matter. Unbeknown to me he had muttered something about not having a pilot's licence. The next thing I knew was the police insisting on taking us to the local police station.

Once the misunderstanding was ironed out both the school authorities and the police could not have been more friendly or helpful. Derek's instructions were clear:

'Leave the aircraft there, tie it down and I'll collect it tomorrow.'

On hearing that there was no more flying Laurence's entire demeanour changed, his confidence reappeared and he was soon arranging our ground transportation. While we were in the station a lady telephoned to say how lucky it was that she had the windows on both sides of her apartment open as I had flown through it. Another claimed to have seen the pilots on the wing changing places just before the landing.

'A little surprise can produce the most amazing witnesses,' smiled the officer in charge. 'Do you know, we even had reports of an aircraft flying through the railway station and of one following a bus,' he continued.

'Goodness gracious,' we replied.

Even Derek was remarkably understanding when we telephoned him. All that remained was for Laurence to explain to his parents that we would not be home in time for dinner.

'You're not riding around in that little car of his?' enquired his mother suspiciously.

'No, Mother,' he replied truthfully.

My navigation was not as good as I thought and Derek made ever increasing demands on always knowing our exact position and always being ready for a forced landing. As for aerobatics, a vertical climb really had to be vertical with each wing being checked against the horizon during the climb. I learned to use aileron drag to assist in stall turns with an exit absolutely vertically downwards. I was even allowed to open the throttle at the bottom of the dive to produce enough energy for the next manoeuvre. A speciality of Derek's was the clover leaf. It consisted of four consecutive loops with a 90 degree aileron turn in each of the downward segments. I had to align the aircraft on a landmark to ensure that each of the sections was precisely correct, the aim being to hit one's own slipstream on the way down. I lost my fear of inverted spins as Derek convinced me it was difficult to get into an inverted spin by accident, and demonstrated this until I believed him. He could not convince me that I would not fall out of the cockpit during negative-G aerobatics. I could manage inverted manoeuvres, even outside turns that, to start with, felt as though I had to push the rudder the wrong way. I also began to understand just how difficult it was to perform smooth slow rolls as all the controls needed to be in constant motion.

Derek was already beginning to talk about competition aerobatics as there was a special category for low time pilots. I could not overcome my fear of falling out and begged in vain to be allowed to wear a parachute.

'Just remember you're part of the aeroplane,' said Derek. The parachute was obviously against his credo. The problem was that whatever I promised myself on the ground it was never the same in the air. The inch of movement as the straps took up the strain seemed like a mile, and there was my constant fear of the quick release mechanism failing, catapulting me into oblivion. It was hardly surprising that I always hurried through negative-G manoeuvres and this was going to limit any competition performance.

Apart from these lessons a favourite pastime was to engage in dogfights at 4,000 ft. near Stevenage.

Dogfighting was irresponsible, possibly illegal, but enormous fun. We sincerely hoped we were out of earshot of Panshanger where Derek's sharp ears would have detected our goings-on. Naturally we were concerned about collision and overstraining our aircraft. Nevertheless we whizzed around in ever-tightening circles, climbing and diving until someone broke off. The Taylorcraft acquitted itself remarkably well in climb and turns but it was not stressed for aerobatics. The pilot flying the Tiger Moth could always roll on his back and dive vertically knowing that he would not be followed. It certainly sharpened our flying skills.

Then, I had my friends to take flying. Derek insisted on removing the control column from the front cockpit on the grounds of safety. He insisted on this precaution even if the occupant was a pilot. This made sharing the cost of a flight a less attractive proposition. However, I had taken the precaution of removing a control column from a crashed Tiger Moth and kept this as a spare at home. This control column could easily be slipped into the leg of a flying suit. I suspect that Derek knew perfectly well what we were doing in view of the extraordinary number of my passengers who appeared to suffer from stiff legs.

Indeed, it was Derek who told us the story of the RAF instructor whose pupil refused to go solo. Each time he was asked if he was ready the pupil requested another circuit. The instructor consulted with his fellow instructors and together they worked out a plan. Next day, while flying and approaching the airfield the instructor bent down, pulled out his control column, waved it over his head so that his pupil could see it clearly and threw it overboard. He then sat back for the pupil to complete the circuit. Moments later, and to his surprise, he felt a tap on his shoulder. He turned around and to his horror saw his student waving his own control column in the air and then throwing it overboard.

'Bail out,' he instructed the student and tried to help the pupil bail out by standing on the wing. Needless, to say he

fell off and descended gracefully by parachute. To his surprise
he noticed the Tiger Moth completing the circuit and landing
uneventfully. Flushed with anger but tinged with relief at the
student's miraculous safe arrival, he demanded an explanation
as the student climbed out of the cockpit.

'But Sir,' he protested, 'I only copied what you did and
that was only my spare control column.'

After flying in an open cockpit any aircraft with a cabin
was going to be a luxury, particularly in the winter. I looked
forward to not having to wear a flying suit and goggles, and
not worrying about losing maps overboard. Open cockpit
flying required a careful map-folding technique to prevent
the slipstream catching it as the pilot was trying to re-fold it
in the air.

The Taylorcraft was a high wing monoplane with side by
side seating. It was strictly utilitarian and noisy, but the cabin
was enclosed and we sat next to each other. It also had brakes
of a sort. For the first time I had to use my left hand to
operate the control column leaving the right for the central
throttle. The control inputs required were far greater than I
was used to and it felt a bit like stirring a pudding – not that I
had yet tried that exercise. The aircraft was surprisingly
manoeuvrable and even performed quite well in dogfights
with Tiger Moths although it was not aerobatic. Landing
required a rather special technique as the aircraft had a
tendency to float serenely two feet above the runway defying
all attempts by the pilot to contact terra firma before the
boundary hedge. What was needed was almost painful back
pressure on the control column to make any semblance of a
three point landing. This sturdy workhorse was to carry me
through many hours of flying.

Sharing our hangar was an immaculate privately owned Hornet Moth that I had always admired. This pre-war biplane tourer also featured side by side seating and while peering in through the window I was surprised by a tap on my back, 'Nice, isn't she?' smiled a pleasant faced man.

'Yes, it's splendid.'

'Would you like to fly in it?' he asked.

'Yes, please,' came the instant reply.

I entered the cockpit on the passenger side, but this was not what my host had in mind.

'You take the left-hand seat,' he suggested.

Any semblance to the Tiger Moth or Taylorcraft vanished as I sat on leather covered seats and admired the wooden framed dashboard and well fitted carpet. The cockpit resembled a luxury touring car of the 1930s. Even the doors had chrome plated handles. The aircraft boasted a self-starter and brakes that I was assured occasionally worked.

In the air the Hornet handled with all the sweetness of the Tiger Moth yet it was at least 15 m.p.h. faster and far, far quieter. Sitting at the controls watching the Hertfordshire countryside float underneath conjured visions of country houses, long summer days, cucumber sandwiches and endless free time. In fact it seemed the epitome of the hedonistic society of its era. Of course, the reality was different but this delightful aircraft had a feel-good factor that made it a pleasure to fly. Subsequent journeys in Hornet Moths always had this effect on me. Geoffrey de Haviland must have felt the same way as he used one for his own personal transport.

★     ★     ★

*Winter flying at Panshanger.*

Despite the occasional unexpected adventure my student friends kept up their demands for flights and my experience grew. It was always pleasant to return to Croydon and to fly a Tiger Moth down to the south coast. Meanwhile at Panshanger, Austers became available. The Auster was very similar to a Taylorcraft but with a larger cabin that could hold three. A more powerful version could even carry four and this made the economics of expense sharing even more attractive.

'This lever by my left ear is to control the flaps,' I explained to a particularly nervous passenger on the approach. 'Watch what happens as I pull it down,' I suggested, trying to distract him from the rapidly approaching runway. Unfortunately, the ratchet that held it in place was bent or worn. 'Thwack!', with a sudden crash the flaps flew back under the aerodynamic pressure and the aircraft dropped like a lift with a broken cable. Full throttle saved the day, and as we rather shakily climbed away for another attempt my ashen faced passenger yelled into my right ear:

'I don't care what you call that bloody lever, just leave it alone until you've got me on the ground.'

The Auster was a popular club aircraft and was also operated by the Luton Flying Club where we were made welcome by Fred Pinchin. Luton Aerodrome was on the gentle slope of a green covered field that sat on top of a hill overlooking the Vauxhall car works and the town of Luton. The grassy slopes were ideal for picnics while prospective passengers awaited their turn to fly.

I was checked out by Barrie Radley who had been a test pilot for Percivals. Many of their splendid aircraft had been built at Luton. Barrie had just returned from the Middle East where he had been instructing on recently purchased Jet Provosts.

'At least the Auster hasn't got ejection seats,' he informed me as we strolled towards the club aircraft. This seemed a somewhat unnecessary piece of information. As if reading my thoughts he continued:

'Where I've just been the minute we started spins and recovery procedures the buggers would eject – it gives one quite a fright.'

I assured Barrie that I would not even consider ejecting, but there was a problem with the seating – at least as far as I was concerned. Like the Taylorcraft the Auster could only be landed neatly with the stick right back in the pit of my stomach. Half-hearted measures simply produced a series of porpoise-like leaps across the field that demoralised potential

passengers who took a keen interest in the landings carried
out in front of them. The trouble was that the chief pilot of
Auster was rather more than 6 ft. tall and the aircraft
appeared to have been designed around his bulk. There was
little or no seat adjustment so that pilots of my more
compact build had trouble seeing over the dashboard and
reaching the rudder pedals. The vision problem was easily
solved by a cushion but the second cushion to help reach the
pedals posed more of a problem. If the cushion was too
thick, the stick could not be pulled back sufficiently to
achieve a neat three point landing. After some trial and
error I worked out the ideal combination and always kept
them with me. They were to lead to the loss of my first true
love.

Caroline was simply gorgeous. She had an attractive face
that always seemed to carry a languid smile with an affected
slightly bored expression. She had a marvellous figure and
long legs that she displayed with consummate skill. Caroline
modelled and aimed for the film world. At parties she would
normally be seen seated in a prominent position smoking
with an extremely long cigarette holder. To my teenaged eyes
she was the epitome of sophistication. At twenty-one,
Caroline was a couple of years older than me but in life
experience there was a generation gap. Caroline was simply
out of reach. Needless to say she was pursued by countless
admirers who felt that she was the answer to mankind's
dreams. Caroline thought so too! As a mere student with a
rather small car it seemed impossible to compete with all
these mature adults with their smart sports cars. Then
inspiration struck. Not many people flew aircraft and I didn't
actually have to tell her that it wasn't my aeroplane.

'Next Sunday I'm taking the plane for a little trip from Luton, would you like a ride?' I asked.

'You mean in your own private aircraft? Caroline enquired her eyes visibly larger.

At least she seemed impressed.

'Actually, it's quite small,' I replied truthfully, avoiding the question of ownership and implying great modesty. Her companion glared daggers.

'Do I have to wear special clothes?' Caroline enquired.

'Oh no,' I smiled. 'Just dress comfortably.'

'I'm looking forward to it,' smiled Caroline, and uncrossed her legs.

I booked the aircraft for the Sunday morning, prayed for good weather and waited for the great day. It was a bright cheerful morning. Reeking of aftershave I collected Caroline who appeared not to notice the shortcomings of my ancient car.

'Have you been flying long?' Caroline enquired with a touch of nervousness in her voice.

'Ever since I left school,' came the truthful, if evasive, reply. 'By the way, you can't smoke in the aircraft,' I said with as much authority as I could muster.

'Not even in the cabin, or the toilet?'

We obviously had a misunderstanding about what was meant by small. Maybe I had overdone the false modesty bit.

'Caroline, the aircraft only seats three people,' I explained. 'It's quite comfortable but a trifle noisy.' I smiled back.

'Oh, I see,' came the slightly uneasy reply.

Then she smiled again – perhaps there was still hope. I breezed into the Luton Flying Club as if I owned it, and proudly displayed the Auster together with the controls.

Caroline's looks had not gone unnoticed in the Club House and several helpers came to assist with her safety harness. Caroline's languid smile had reappeared as she looked at her audience and crossed her legs. That was a mistake in the narrow confines of the Auster's cockpit and the rest of the damage was done by the control column. She only lost her composure for an instant although the smile had a more frosty tone.

A familiar face appeared at my side.

'Glad to see you here,' said Derek. 'I'm taking the Hawk over to Old Warden for maintenance. Follow me over and bring me back. Don't worry about sheep on the airfield, I'll deal with them,' he added.

'Who is that strange man?' Caroline asked suspiciously. 'And what was he saying about sheep?'

'Oh, he's a friend, asking a favour. Anyway it will be an interesting flight,' I replied, hoping that I would be able to keep the Hawk in sight as Old Warden would not be easy to find, and getting lost would not be a good way to impress my girl friend or please Derek.

'Funny way to ask a favour,' Caroline muttered.

The Miles Hawk Major was a beautiful open cockpit monoplane of the late pre-war era. It was later to form an important part of my aviation experience. My immediate concern was that Derek's engine was already running and I hoped he would wait for me.

'Clear prop!' I called, and pressed the starter button. A muffled explosion came from the front followed by a noise like three steam engines all running simultaneously. I hurriedly switched off. The helpers were pointing at the engine.

'Don't worry,' I smiled. 'We seem to have a minor problem with the exhaust. We'll borrow another aircraft.'

Helpers rushed to assist Caroline out of the cockpit and within minutes she was strapped in the other Auster. Derek was waiting with his engine ticking over. The moment I climbed in alongside Caroline I sensed something was wrong and as I sat down I realised what it was. I had forgotten my cushions. My manly pride forbade me explaining my predicament. I had no forward vision and could just about reach the pedals with my toes. However I could see perfectly out of the side window and I was quite used to weaving from side to side when taxiing Tiger Moths. When the tail came up during flight I would be able to see forward. The engine ran sweetly.

'Is everything all right?' my passenger enquired, with a tinge of apprehension.

'Relax, this is going to be an experience,' I smiled back, more prophetically than I realised. We weaved from side to side, watched Derek take-off and noisily followed him into the air. Caroline was ashen grey, holding her seat.

'Watch the view,' I shouted above the engine noise. 'It's just like a magic carpet.'

'It's a noisy, rattling and shaking carpet,' came the reply.

My main concerns were trying to impress Caroline who was sitting on my right and not losing sight of the Hawk that Derek was flying on my left. To get lost over the featureless Hertfordshire countryside would be a sure way of losing the confidence of both my new found girl and my flying instructor. Slowly Caroline's tense features relaxed into her captivating languid smile and she began to look from side to side and enjoy the view.

Suddenly I became aware of Caroline's hand on the inside of my thigh. I couldn't believe it, I glanced quickly to the right. Gone was the languid smile. I saw her rounded passion filled eyes, her pouting lips and she was gasping with rapid small breaths. I thought of the aftershave adverts. 'Perhaps this stuff really works,' I muttered to myself.

Caroline couldn't speak; the only sensible thing to do was to release my straps and to take her into my arms, which was what she obviously wanted. I had seen this in the films. With my left hand I felt for the quick release. Just then Caroline found her voice. It was not the gentle cooing I expected. In fact it was more like 'Aaaahgh !!!' A warbling noise that grew both in pitch and intensity finishing with a high pitched screech like new chalk on a blackboard. Her left hand was no longer on my thigh, but pointing through my side window.

Derek had become bored with flying at our slow speed and had decided to put on a small aerobatic display. He was now a few yards away on my left, upside down and waving. In front of Caroline's horrified gaze he let the nose drop then plummeted vertically downwards like a World War II dive-bomber. Immediately beneath us lay Old Warden aerodrome.

'Can we land soon,' beseeched my passenger. 'I'm not really enjoying this.'

'We'll be there shortly,' I replied reassuringly.

In fact, I had been looking in vain for Old Warden for the last two or three minutes but I need not have worried. Derek, like a Stuka dive bomber, was hurtling downwards towards the grass airfield. I could not see any sheep on it but Derek's low level pass would have scattered any that were there. At our more leisurely pace I followed Derek onto the circuit.

'This lever controls the flaps,' I explained to my pale passenger, 'We may bounce once or twice but that's quite normal. As the field is short we will land close to the hedge.'

If I had been more experienced I would have flown a curved descent much favoured by Spitfire pilots and others with lack of good forward vision on the approach. However, I was so worried about overshooting that I dragged the poor Auster low and slow along its final approach with no forward vision. Well ahead of us Derek was just skimming the boundary hedge. Looking out of the side window I saw the hedge, then the grass and touched down with the gentlest of bumps. Just as I was congratulating myself the surprised face of a cow appeared alongside the left wing. I had just time to realise that it was a cow not a sheep, when the hedge appeared. I had landed in the field next door! There was no question of stopping. Frantic application of full throttle allowed us to jump the hedge, followed by a most inelegant 'Thud' as we smacked down onto the threshold of Old Warden's runway, straining the undercarriage suspension to its limits.

Ahead Derek was still in with his tail towards us; he could not possibly have seen anything untoward. Caroline's eyes were firmly closed; perhaps she hadn't noticed anything either.

'Wasn't that fun?' I smiled at her.

There was no reply. Instead, an extraordinary transformation had occurred to Caroline's physiognomy. Instead of the languid smile, a deep and ugly scowl had appeared and her chin seemed to have doubled in size. As I taxied in, Derek seemed to be staring at the Auster's undercarriage. However, as Caroline swung her door open he transferred his gaze to my passenger's undercarriage.

'Enjoy the flight?' he solicitously enquired. 'Would you like me to get you a coffee?'

'Just get me a taxi,' hissed Caroline, as she stalked out of my life without a backward glance. Even her legs had grown shorter.

Derek hurried to look after her, and I quickly removed the bits of hedge from the landing gear.

CHAPTER 8

# Across the Channel

FINE WEEKENDS seldom passed without a flight. My student friends rallied round to seek trips and the Auster became very popular. At least two of these passengers became licensed pilots and continued to fly for years after. Around that time I made my first trip across the Channel. It was an excursion, one of the last, from Croydon organised by the Surrey Flying Club. Rather like World War II, the most experienced pilot was to act as navigator and the rest of us were to follow in a fairly loose formation.

'Remember there is a clearly defined Light Aircraft Crossing,' said Tiny. 'I'll be following up the rear in case anyone has trouble. If you have to ditch don't land into the swell and try to drop in tail skid first. You'll probably flip over.'

'Whatever happens don't inflate your life jacket until you're clear of the aircraft,' said Peter. 'Actually your most serious problem is landing on the tarmac runway at Le Touquet. The grass is unsuitable – don't try it, as we lost an aircraft last year that finished up in the river. Slow, slow please.'

It was a memorable day and Le Touquet was to become a popular destination – as it still is – for years afterwards. It also opened our eyes as to what could be achieved with even slower aircraft, such as the Tiger Moth. With its pedestrian cruising speed Le Touquet was still only 1 hour 20 minutes from Croydon.

A little while later I made my first journey alone to Le Touquet, this time flying an Auster with two passengers. While there was nothing remarkable about the journey, there was great sadness that Croydon airport was closing and that the Surrey Flying Club, together with other users of the airport, had to find new homes. It appeared to mark the end of an era in British aviation.

Back at Panshanger I was told that I would be allowed to fly the Miles Hawk Major with which I immediately fell in love. It was owned by a very kind gentleman who did not fly it a great deal himself and it was sometimes moved to Luton. Derek looked after the aircraft and demanded his customary precision from the few pilots who were trusted with it. G-ADWT had been built in 1936 and bore a resemblance to the Magister, on which so many war-time pilots were trained. It was a tandem two-seater open cockpit monoplane with extremely sleek lines. The wheels were cleverly faired in trouser-like extensions that were a hallmark of Miles designs of the period. Other characteristics were the splendid low speed handling, and manoeuvrability, all combined with an excellent performance. It could easily outpace machines with similar engines that were twenty-five years younger. It had relatively small fin and rudder areas and this might have accounted for the *No Spinning* notices that were displayed in both cockpits. Derek appeared to take the messages as a challenge.

'Nonsense,' he snarled. 'Of course you can easily spin and recover. Climb in and we'll see what you can do.'

The flight consisted of climbing to 4,000 ft. and Derek

spinning to the right, recovering, climbing, and then doing the same to the left.

'Back to 4,000 ft. and you do the same,' came my instructions.

The Hawk spun and recovered perfectly well although I could not help but notice how quickly the speed would build up after the recovery and before I raised the nose above the horizon.

'The trouble with the small fin and rudder is that they can be screened from the airflow while side slipping. It has effective flaps so you won't need to side slip on the approach,' Derek said.

The notices were removed and replaced with others saying *No Side Slipping*. Derek insisted that all pilots flying the Hawk were able to demonstrate spins and recovery. Derek's ambition to turn me into a competition aerobatic pilot was boundless. The Hawk Major had a far better performance than the Tiger Moth but I still had not lost my fear of falling out of the cockpit while inverted. Performing negative G-manoeuvres that actually tended to throw me out of the cockpit, straining against the straps, required a great deal of gritting of teeth. The ancient strap-securing mechanism only had to fail and I would be hurled out of the aircraft like an ejector seat. Talking about it on the ground was one thing; hanging upside down a few thousand feet above Hertfordshire was quite another. I begged Derek to change his mind and allow me to wear a parachute, but he was adamant.

'I've told you once and I'm telling you again that you are part of the aircraft,' he stipulated. 'Never forget it, then you will fly properly.'

We were still using speaking tubes for communication, although the installation of a battery powered intercom was promised. The arrival was hastened by an instance that could have been catastrophic. I had a friend who wanted to try aerobatics. We climbed to a safe height, and made sure there were no other aircraft nearby.

'Check harness,' I called down the tube.

'Fine,' came the reply.

I did one loop before I noticed frantic waving from the front cockpit.

'What's the problem?' I enquired.

'My straps are undone,' she screamed, 'I told you to wait.'

It transpired that my passenger had undone her harness believing she could get it really tight by starting again. Fortunately I had not tried a slow roll.

The Hawks' wooden construction and glued joints that were involved cast a shadow over the longevity of the aircraft. This was brought home when the aircraft was being refuelled at Shoreham Airport, where it had been built before the war. The silver-haired gentleman refuelling it remembered actually building the machine twenty-five years previously and added as an afterthought:

'I did not really think it would still be airworthy!'

This did not add to my confidence during aerobatic flight.

It was doubtless the ageing structure and the possible weakening of the glued joints that resulted in the licensing authorities reducing the maximum permissible speed of the aircraft. This was now brought down to 150 miles per hour, a speed that the Hawk could reach in level flight, let alone in aerobatic manoeuvres. It was therefore possible to commence many aerobatic manoeuvres from level flight but the speed limitation was an obvious problem. Of course, we knew there was a safety margin and occasionally used it, but the streamlined shape meant that speed could build up alarmingly quickly. I still do not know how it happened but I must have fallen off the top of a roll. All I vividly remember is the rush of the wind noise during an inverted descent and staring horrorstruck at the rapidly increasing airspeed indicator that was already well past 200 miles per hour and rising by the second. If I had been wearing a parachute I would have used it without any hesitation. Baling out of an inverted aircraft could not have been easier. My instinctive reaction was to pull the stick back and complete the downward half of a loop. This was a sure way to disaster as the speed would build to catastrophic levels. The aircraft already seemed on the verge of breaking up. My instructor had at least instilled in me the need to overcome my dislike of negative-G, to ease the control column forward, raise the nose and half roll to become upright. Of course, easing the stick forward caused me to be forced outwards against the harness that I imagined was creaking – or was it the airframe? I rolled upright, and the nose was eased above the horizon. This time it was positive G that pushed me back into the seat. It was also easier on the airframe that had been built to take much higher positive than negative loads. The speed began to reduce. It seemed to take an hour but I imagine it was all over in a few seconds. I still do not like to think of the speed the aircraft reached. However, the airframe held together.

'Now you see why I won't let you wear a parachute,' smiled Derek.

From the aircraft's point of view he was correct. From the

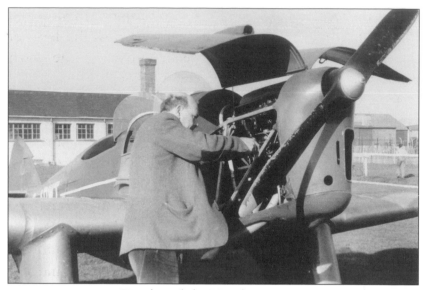

*Derek and the Hawk at Luton.*

pilot's view point I was not convinced. The engineer who inspected the aircraft assured me that there was no permanent harm done. He was wrong: my ambition to take part in aerobatic competitions had vanished.

For touring, general flying and the occasional loop or barrel roll, the Hawk was sheer delight, and I regained my confidence in the machine. One day just after take-off from Luton the engine cut. I quickly changed tanks, aiming for a field, but after a few seconds the engine picked up and behaved perfectly. Luton airport is on the top of a hill and this extra height had saved me the embarrassment of a forced landing. There was no fuel remaining in the left tank which I had used for take-off – the fuel gauge had jammed and was still reading half full. From then on I really did take heed of my instructors' warnings and checked fuel quantities visually, and have done so ever since. This hill also saved the life of one of the local flying instructors who misjudged a slow roll in a Chipmunk and was seen to recover below the level of the airfield. He survived to become one of the most prominent names in British General Aviation.

With my improving expertise I was never short of potential passengers. I became adept at handling the Hawk with its minor eccentricities and began to visit airfields further and further away from our base. Over its twenty-five years it had developed a minor leak in the hydraulically operated flap system. The result was that having lowered the flaps for landing they tended to slowly retract under the influence of air pressure. This meant that my left hand was kept busy continually pumping the landing flaps while also manipulating the throttle. Provided I remembered not to sideslip and to rely on flap for landing it was vice free. Although the idea of competition aerobatics was now well and truly behind me, the occasional roll or a loop on a sunny day was still a great joy to perform. Forced landing practices and the associated excuse for low flying continued to hold its fascination, danger and illicit attractions.

However, there was one challenge that continued to attract both military and civil pilots.

'Flying under bridges is dangerous, illegal, and highly irresponsible endangering not only the pilot but members of the general public,' lectured Tony Richmond.

The steady toll of fatal accidents to pilots who could not resist the lure of these man-made temptations was a sad testimony of the times and showed that he was right. It was apparent that flying under a bridge required detailed planning of the exit route where most of the accidents occurred.

'Don't do it,' Tony continued. 'But if you're so crazy that

you can't resist it for heaven's sake plan the exit route, where you're most likely to crash. Remember that many bridges are over tidal areas and the space available changes from hour to hour. A ship – or even an aircraft – coming the other way is going to cause you embarrassment if you haven't seen it. That's not the only problem. What happens if the bridge spans a gorge like the Clifton Bridge? It's so easy just to concentrate on simply getting under the bridge. If you've got drift correction on the run in, just imagine the turbulence and downdrafts when you try to climb out of the gorge. A Meteor went in last month.'

I never forgot Tony's words. And yet the challenge proved irresistible to some, and both irresistible and fatal to others.

A certain ex-World War I pilot, Major Draper, was informed that although he might have passed his last medical examination the authorities felt that at his advanced age he must have lost the coordination necessary to fly an aircraft. His response was immediate, effective and well publicised. He flew under all of the London bridges and some of them leave little room to spare, particularly at high tide.

At Panshanger, one of the members was taking a new girlfriend for a flight in an Auster. Dispensing with the precaution of wheel chocks he merely set the brakes and got out to hand swing the propeller. Since nothing much seemed to be happening his girlfriend also climbed out – just as the engine fired. The throttle vibrated open, the brakes did not hold and the pilotless aircraft took off. The flight terminated in a ball of fire at the far end of the airfield. Similar mishaps with pilotless aircraft were not unknown. Unfortunately not all mishaps ended without casualty. The Chairman of the Flying Club and three passengers were killed when an engine failed on a twin-engine Miles Germini just after take-off and the aircraft spun into the ground.

It was a tragic lesson that the handling of twin-engine aircraft required special training and skills.

The Auster proved an exceedingly popular club aircraft all over the country. Those with British made Cirrus Minor and more powerful Gipsy Major engines appeared to pre-dominate, until the arrival of the American Lycoming engine which was more powerful still and allowed the aircraft to carry four people. We had one Lycoming engine Auster at the Club that was always in heavy demand and I looked forward to getting my hands on it. The Lycoming engine suffered from one drawback. It was relatively easy to start when cold but once the engine was hot, starting it could be difficult as it flooded at the slightest provocation. As a result, Club Members took to leaving the engine running while changing pilots and passengers, and special care and briefing was necessary to avoid mishaps with the propeller and possible malfunction of brakes.

'This one's a beaut! Take my passengers clear of the prop, climb in and I'll look after your passengers,' was my briefing from the pilot flying it before me. Having climbed aboard and settled down behind the controls, I taxied out to line up along the grass runway, watched by the rest of the Club who were lounging outside the Club House which was parallel to the runway separated by a distance of about 50 yards. I opened the throttle of this sprightly mount leading with the customary bootful of left rudder that one applied to counteract the effect of engine torque and the asymmetrical aerodynamic effects of the rotating propeller. The result was dramatic.

Instead of surging along the runway the aircraft spun around its left wheel like a startled deer and headed straight for the Club House and the row of deck chairs. Of course I cut the throttle immediately and returned to the holding point to gather my thoughts. Only then did it dawn on me that American engines rotated in the opposite direction to their British counterparts. Austers had self-starters but hand swinging was still occasionally necessary. If you stood in front of a British engine aircraft and turned to face it the propeller turned clockwise so that you used your right arm for hand swinging. The American engines rotated anti-clockwise which meant that they had to be hand swung with the left hand – and hand swinging these models was considerably more difficult. Naturally, the effect of the torque was exactly opposite to that which I had experienced in all previous air-craft I had flown and explained the unexpected response to the application of full left rudder. When I lined up for my next attempt I could not but help notice that the Club Members were no longer seated and, in fact, appeared crouched ready for another sprint. Naturally, opening the throttle and feeding a progressive amount of right rudder produced a completely normal take-off. It was yet another important lesson to show how apparently similar aircraft can behave so very differently and that a check-out, or at least a thorough briefing, is always an investment – never a waste of time.

At Panshanger Derek's cadre of young pilots was gaining confidence. Among them was Harvey who was some fifteen years older than the younger members; he had served in World War II, and had sufficient self-confidence not to be intimidated by our instructor. Harvey had a relaxed approach to aviation.

'I'm flying for enjoyment, not for yet more work,' he used to state.

This attitude could not have been more different from the precision of technique demanded by Derek. In despair, Derek used to complain:

'Harvey, the landing is meant to be the termination of the flight – not the end of the aircraft!'

From Harvey's point of view if there was no significant damage on landing then all was well. If the landing happened to be at the correct airfield then it was an added bonus! A parting of the ways was inevitable.

The standard compass issued to British aircraft of the era was known as the P-11 and it was a beautiful piece of equipment. A substantial precision-made device, it occupied a prominent position on the floor, or in the roof of the cabin. There was a rotating bezel on which you set your desired magnetic heading and then manoeuvred the aircraft until the north facing needle was against the north mark of the bezel. There were two parallel lines that were aligned with the compass needle and showed the slightest divergence. This allowed magnetic headings to be flown with precision – provided you had set the heading correctly to start with. Of course, tales abounded of pilots who had flown 180 degrees or 90 degrees to their intended heading, and there was the story of the Chipmunk pilot who found himself in Holland instead of Cambridge. I suspect that Harvey found the setting of the magnetic heading somewhat irksome which may account for some of his remarkable unplanned excursions.

Harvey was always great fun to be with and we decided to take two aircraft from Panshanger to Le Touquet, landing at

Lympne for customs. Harvey was flying his own Tiger Moth by now and set off first as the Hawk was so much faster. Fortunately, we took off while he was still in sight as he seemed to be headed for Moscow! With the extra speed of the Hawk we were able to overhaul him and point that he should follow us. All went well as we came over Lympne and following standard non-radio procedure I looked at the signal square to see which runway was being used. We landed, taxied to the Control Tower and climbed its steps to pay the landing fee. The controller remembered the Hawk from days gone by and was talking about the machine, and looked up as my girlfriend came through the door.

'Jesus,' he muttered, and the colour drained from his face.

I'm not sure which of us was more startled by this unusual greeting until we followed the direction of his gaze. Harvey's aircraft was lined up with a short grass runway that was some 60 degrees to the one in use and which crossed it about halfway along. This meant that Harvey was not only likely to collide with the aircraft that was approaching to land on the correct runway but that he was also 60 degrees out of wind, which in a Tiger Moth was going to require a great deal of skill.

Naturally the controller grabbed his large signalling lamp and shone a steady red light, but the Tiger Moth continued its approach. Muttering under his breath, the controller rushed onto the balcony and proceeded to send a series of red flares skyward. This was, of course, a mandatory order not to land. The aircraft on the approach to the correct runway broke off but Harvey was so busy coping with the self-made cross wind that he did not have time to see the red lights, nor the pyrotechnic display. Instead, he appeared to make a landing on his left wheel, left wing tip and tail skid, then bounced, repeated the procedure on the other side of the aircraft, then bounced back onto both main wheels with the tail high as it crossed the main runway and disappeared behind the hedge into the glider park. Fortunately, Harvey had cut the magneto switches for when we all sprinted round the corner to find the wreckage, there was the Tiger Moth standing sweetly on its nose with its tail high up in the air but with no apparent damage. Several of the glider pilots who had thrown themselves in various directions were dusting themselves down. Harvey's girlfriend in the front cockpit was quite easy to reach but poor Harvey was some six feet in the air. I noticed the controller reloading his pistol and thought for an awful moment that execution might have been on his mind. His facial expression suggested that is what he was contemplating but it became apparent that the controller had several matters that he wished to discuss with Harvey. We thought it prudent to lead Ann away.

'Never mind, darling,' she called out. 'We've known worse.'

We extended our stay at Le Touquet in order to allow minor repairs to be carried out to Harvey's wing tip, as his arrival there had not been without incident either. On our way back to Lympne I wondered what reception awaited us. As soon as the controller noticed Harvey's aircraft in the circuit he scrambled the fire engine. I am told that the controller continued to carry out this precaution for months to come whenever Harvey's aircraft was seen in his circuit.

Harvey was however able to land at Lympne without the fire engine when he arrived as navigator in a Percival Proctor, owned by a friend of his, Simon. The Proctor was a low

wing monoplane with a fixed undercarriage that held four
people and demonstrated a remarkable turn of speed: some
150 m.p.h. although it was rumoured to have rather
unpleasant stalling characteristics. Harvey and Simon were
planning a day trip to Le Touquet and as Harvey had been
there before he was acting as navigator. The trip from
Lympne to Le Touquet should have taken about twenty
minutes on a south-easterly heading and as the weather was
good they should not have been out of sight of land for any
appreciable time. The conversation in the aircraft must have
been interesting and far too involved for anyone to keep an
eye on the compass that must by now have been pointing in
a southerly direction. After twenty minutes neither appeared
to realise that they had not reached their destination nor
appreciated the significance that all they could see was water.
Still the conversation continued and the compass by now
had slowly swung to a south-westerly heading carrying
the aircraft towards the Western Approaches, and eventually
the United States, if it maintained the heading and had
unlimited fuel.

Fortunately, they did not maintain the heading as the
compass slowly but surely swung to a westerly and then a
north-westerly direction. By the time a coastline appeared,
nearly an hour after departure, neither of the crew
appreciated the significance of their northerly heading.
Neither party appeared concerned about the time they had
been over the water.

'There it is,' shouted Harvey, 'I can see the river.'

'I can see the field,' called Simon, 'but there doesn't seem
to be much happening on it.'

'Don't worry,' said Harvey, 'They're probably all at lunch.

I can see the coast, I can see the river, and the aerodrome is in the right place.'

'I can't see the signal square,' said Simon.

'Never mind,' said Harvey. 'Just land into wind.'

They taxied towards a derelict looking control tower.

'Funny,' said Simon, 'I can't see any other aircraft. It looks very shabby.'

'Well,' said Harvey, 'I'm afraid the French are a bit like that. Never mind, we'll have a good lunch.'

They switched off, and a man on a bicycle approached.

'*Bonjour, monsieur, comment allez-vous,*' smiled Harvey.

'Get orf me bleeding land,' came the unexpected reply, with a slight Yorkshire accent.

'What do you mean,' said Harvey. 'This is Le Touquet Airport.'

'Le Touquet, fiddlesticks!' came the reply, 'You're in Christchurch, and this aerodrome has been closed for three years. Now get the 'ell out of 'ere or I'll call the police. Your nearest airport is Hurn, Bournemouth, just a few miles west,' said the cyclist, 'and if you don't know which direction that is, jus' keep the sun on yer left,' he added as an afterthought, as he cycled away.

CHAPTER 9

# The London-Paris Air Race

Most of our thoughts were now concentrated by an announcement that the *Daily Mail* was to celebrate the 50th Anniversary of Bleriot's Channel crossing in 1909 by sponsoring an air race from London to Paris. The race was from Marble Arch in London to the Arc de Triomphe in Paris or the other way round. Competitors could make more than one run in either direction; only the fastest time counted. From the outset it was apparent that private entrants could not compete with the muscle of government or industrial organisations and so unofficial classes of entrants were effectively created. The RAF, and later, the French air force, also became involved.

I was struggling in a laboratory surrounded by tormented electric motors when I felt a hand on my shoulder.

'We're going to do the Paris air race,' announced Paul, a fellow student and a future distinguished professor.

'Who?'

'You and I,' he replied.

'Where on earth will we find the money and what transport can we use?' I asked incredulously.

'You look after the aviation and I'll deal with the ground transportation,' smiled Paul and sauntered off with the confident air of one who had already accomplished all he required. Paul was a skilled rally driver and one of the fastest

*Preparing the Hawk for the London-Paris air race.*

individuals on the road provided that he stayed on it. It was unlikely that anyone would beat us on the ground, but that was only a small part of the journey. For our part we approached manufacturers of jet aircraft and helicopters, who were all very polite but none could be found willing to provide the necessary transport free. Ours was obviously going to be an economy run. We had also made another discovery. No matter how quickly we drove, a well ridden motorcycle could beat us through the crowded streets of central London. Fortunately, Paul was able to persuade the very generous managing director of Lambrettas to provide us with two high performance motor-scooters, and expert competition riders, both in London and Paris. We were going to use the Miles Hawk Major for aerial transportation. Since we had no access to a helicopter Croydon was the nearest airfield with customs that we could use. By now Croydon was closing but thanks to the good offices of a friend we obtained permission to use it for the air race. The price to pay was taking the friend on the first run!

Finding an airport close to the centre of Paris was not so

straightforward as we had no radio equipment at all. At long last we thought we had obtained permission to use Issy that had now become the Paris Heli-Port.

*'Mon dieu, c'est impossible!'*

In a torrent of French the Commandant of the Paris Heli-Port hastily withdrew his permission to land when he discovered that we carried no radio and we were not a helicopter anyway. We were obliged to use Toussous le Noble, an aerodrome near Versailles that would add a great deal to the journey time as it was a long road journey to the Arc de Triomphe. I should not have been concerned as the French riders had planned an amazingly fast route into Paris in which traffic lights, or any other artificial impediment to the rapid progress of a fast moving vehicle, were to be totally ignored. For our part while practising in London, we had discovered that in the suburban areas a high performance car could beat the scooters, but it took a few hair-raising episodes to persuade Lambrettas that this was truly the case. The specially tuned Lambrettas were unbeatable in traffic and so the change over from Lambretta to A.C. Bristol and modified M.G. was planned near Balham in South London.

To be on the safe side we flew the Hawk from Croydon to Toussous the day before the race as I had never flown this distance let alone the route before. This was also the first time that I had flown more than 70 miles over open water and it was obvious that one navigational mistake could undo months of careful planning and practice. We made a careful reconnaissance of the French coast either side of our planned crossing point so that on the race day I would know exactly where landfall had been made and could then make a suitable correction to our heading to bring me on track for Toussous.

When we eventually found Toussous we got the shock of our lives. There appeared to be several aerodromes all close together with overlapping circuits and the chaos was fantastic. Apart from nearly ramming a helicopter, landing at the wrong aerodrome, and narrowly winning a dog fight in the landing race, our arrival at Toussous was almost uneventful, the only untoward occurrence being the antics of a helicopter pilot who patiently waited for our wheels to touch before performing a lightning take-off. Small wonder that I made one of the worst landings of my flying career and nearly finished up in the restaurant where the French director of Lambretta's was awaiting us with a splendid lunch.

'Come eere kwik, vee do ze rest,' he smiled.

On the way back, we relaxed, and promptly got lost over the rather featureless countryside to the north-west of Paris that added 40 minutes to our return leg. This was a warning that we heeded.

The race day dawned fair. Almost all our student friends had turned out as helpers to block strategic crossings at the appropriate time, a friendly level crossing keeper had promised to keep the gates open to the last possible second (or to close them immediately after us if we had police escort). In practising for last minute dashes through closing railway crossing gates we had made a disconcerting discovery. 60 m.p.h. equates to 88 ft. per second, so if you mark a point 80 yards (240 ft.) before the gate, you should be through it about three seconds later. It took but one hair-raising episode to realise our mistake. Getting through the gate was indeed useful, but it was passing the *second* gate on the far side of the tracks that was truly essential! Another friend was to have the Hawk with its engine running ready for take-off at Croydon.

A running jump and we were both seated on the back of the scooters ridden by Lambretta's chief road tester and head mechanic. I shall never forget those few terrifying minutes as we cornered at impossible speeds, silencers scraping the ground. I wondered if we should ever reach Croydon, but not for long. I vividly remember falling clear as, with an appalling crash, the machine rolled over in a shower of sparks and dust and then I hit my head on a car. While I was sitting in the road with a ripped flying suit surveying the wreckage of a Lambretta and my rider emerging from underneath the car with which we had collided, I was collected by our back-up transport and the 'wall of death' act started all over again. We just made the level crossing as the gates were beginning to close. Paul's rev counter was in the red zone in top gear. There was one point at which I knew we would have to stop. To save time we had arranged to enter Croydon airport through a north-facing side gate that led straight onto the airfield. It meant crossing a 4-lane main road with a central division. Although there was a gap in the division, and we were facing the airfield, the traffic on the main road was hidden by hedges. This was one road we could not block. I braced myself for the heavy braking but I had reckoned without Paul.

'Wow!' was about all I could mutter, as we shot straight across the road flat out in top gear.

'The faster we go, the less likely we'll hit anything,' shouted Paul as we tore through the gate at close to 100 m.p.h. I've no idea of the chaos we left behind on the main road. Seventeen minutes from Marble Arch (some seventeen miles all through town) found us seated in the Hawk ready for take-off.

The flight to Paris was the least eventful part of the journey. Without taxing the engine beyond its normal cruising speed we landed at Toussous 1 hour 30 minutes later. Sixty years after the Hawk Major was built there are a still a number of light aircraft that would be happy to match its performance. The rest of the journey to the Arc de Triomphe was a kaleidoscope of screeching tyres, jumped traffic signals, and blaring horns. No other student entry had come anywhere near us in terms of time. We made an uneventful return to Croydon for an attempt the next day to better our time, but this time Paul was to accompany me to Paris. Although there was no mishap with the scooters the engine of the MG seized in a spectacular fashion. The time was one second faster than the previous day!

Lambretta's were amazingly enthusiastic about the performance of their machines and happy with the associated publicity. We were loaned one of the high performance scooters until our return next day.

'Let's see how fast it goes,' yelled Paul as we snaked up the Champs-Élysées at ridiculous speed. Since the machine had a rev counter but no speedometer we were obliged to peer into car windows to read their speed.

Then it was Paul's turn to sit on the back.

'Ever ridden one before?' he enquired with a touch of anxiety in his voice.

'No, but I'll learn quickly,' I replied.

I was in fact quite capable of riding the scooter, but I thought I would make him sweat a bit after his terrifying display on the Champs-Élysées.

*Arrival at the Arc de Triomphe.*

I headed for Montmartre where I intended to seek my revenge displaying my skills at high speed cornering and a few tricks I had learnt from the Lambretta boys.

'Jesus!' muttered Paul as we commenced our high speed descent from the top of the hill.

Ahead the road straightened for a few yards and I opened the throttle fully. With the benefit of the steep hill the scooter hurtled towards a left hand corner. Too late I realised that under-braking we were skipping from one cobblestone to another and not slowing down much. We were not going to get round the corner. The diners on the pavement of the corner restaurant had also come to similar conclusions and had begun to scatter as we crashed between the tables, chairs and serving trolleys. We were ruefully surveying the wreckage and wondering what it would cost when we became aware that everyone was cheering. We still had our competition numbers on the machine and guests and management were unanimous that as we had already entered the restaurant we should stay for dinner. There was in fact no serious damage and everyone in Paris had entered the spirit of the race. Bleriot, after all, was a Frenchman.

On the next day the French air force joined the fray flying, of course, from Paris to London. I suspect this was a last minute affair relying on flair and ingenuity as a substitute for practice. A glamorous lady was to be the competitor whisked by Vautour fighter bomber from Villacoublay near Paris to Biggin Hill for onward transmission by helicopter. Biggin Hill airfield sits on top of a hill and has a splendid main runway that can accommodate most jets. Nearby Kenley also sits on an adjacent hill and had been closed for years. Its runway was very short, and was only used by air cadets for basic gliding training. It was an easy mistake to make as the Vautour approached London flat out at low level. A flight sergeant and his cadets were having a quiet cup of tea at Kenley when the Vautour suddenly hit their runway in a mass of screeching tyres, jet blast and blue smoke. The cadets threw themselves to safety as the Vautour careered off the end of the runway. They were still dusting themselves down when the helicopter from Biggin Hill hurtled over, picked up the crew and disappeared towards Battersea. I don't know how they recovered the aircraft.

For our part, we set off from Toussous for Lympne, in Kent, where we had to clear customs as Luton had none at the time. Just at the north-west of Paris we had to take violent evasive action to avoid hitting a Hawker Hunter jet that was travelling flat out at tree top level, and must have left a trail of shattered eardrums if not window panes between London and Paris. The trusty Hawk carried us back without incident, a truly remarkable aircraft.

The London Paris Air Race had rekindled the spirit of adventure in both countries. People travelled by the most unusual methods and it also marked the arrival of the vertical take-off jet aircraft. Seeing a crowd of well dressed dignitaries waiting for its arrival in the Paddington marshalling yards was a unique experience. Anyone associated with aviation could foresee the effect of the jet blast upon layers of coal dust and soot that must have been deposited over generations. As expected, officialdom was promptly transformed into the Black and White Minstrel show but the vertical take-off aircraft had arrived. The most popular route for those using high performance jet aircraft was a motorcycle ride to the Battersea Heliport, a helicopter to Biggin Hill, a rapid flight to Villacoublay, near Paris, followed by another helicopter ride to Issi and then a motorcycle trip. Times of under 45 minutes from Marble Arch to the Arc de Triomphe were recorded and would be hard to beat today. I believe that the organisers had inserted a regulation to the effect that all speed limits and regulations were to be obeyed!

We continued to fly the Hawk for nearly another year until the owner was obliged to sell it. I am told that it now resides in a museum in the United States. In August that year I took an Auster from Croydon to Le Touquet. While there was nothing special about this trip I was sad to see such a historic landmark in British aviation closing its doors after serving the first two generations of human powered flight.

CHAPTER 10

# Biggin Hill

FOLLOWING THE demise of Croydon the Surrey Flying Club had moved to Biggin Hill where it was now known as the Surrey and Kent Flying Club. It occupied quite spacious facilities on the civilian side of Biggin Hill and ran a mixed fleet of aircraft.

Although I still continued to fly and enjoy Tiger Moths I was introduced to its replacement, the Chipmunk. It seemed complete luxury. It had an enclosed cockpit with a sliding canopy, brakes and a self-starter. Unlike the Tiger Moth and Hawk the pilot, or pupil, sat in front and enjoyed a better view. Some of the Chipmunks were just being converted from military to civil standards. The military version had a cartridge starter, whereas in civilian mode an electric self-starter was installed. The Chipmunk was an absolutely joy to fly. It was rumoured that if mistreated and spun for any length of time, the spin could flatten, a situation from which one could only recover by getting the nose firmly down and going through standard recovery procedures. Popular advice suggested that if you were unlucky enough to enter a flat spin at low altitude you sat back and awaited the crash, praying that you could walk away from it, as the rate of descent was relatively low. Indeed, there were rumours of several Chipmunks descending in this manner in the Nile delta without serious injury. In fact, I found the Chipmunk to be virtually vice free. It possessed all the control response of the Tiger Moth and yet was far more comfortable to fly and easier to operate. Although it lacked the performance of the Hawk Major it was hard to beat for enjoying the pure pleasure of flight. Once again fellow students and friends flocked to fly in the Chipmunk and appeared to enjoy being thrown around the sky in it. It was an aircraft I always wanted to own but that was to take another thirty years.

It was around this time that I flew my first American aircraft, a Piper Cub. It was considered one of the most popular light aircraft ever built and it was easy to see why. It was a thoroughly utilitarian machine designed for hard work. It could be flown off rough fields without a murmur of discontent and possessed, in Super Club form, a tremendous rate of climb that allowed it to be operated out of small strips surrounded by obstacles. It could also be landed in a remarkably short distance. In the Piper Cub the passenger sat behind the pilot and the side of the fuselage opened out like a clam shell which permitted easy entry and egress.

It was in a Piper Cub that I entered my first Breakfast Patrol. The general concept was, and probably still is, that a defending aerodrome challenges all comers to enter its circuit and land without having their registration numbers written down by the crews of the defending aircraft. Over the years a series of safety features have been incorporated to prevent some of the wilder manoeuvres that used to take place. Even then, it was appreciated that a safe haven of the aerodrome circuit must exist to allow arriving aircraft to make a normal descent. Before that point virtually anything went – and quite often did.

If you were attempting to fly a slow aircraft like a Tiger

Moth into a defended zone two approaches were favoured and both were relatively risky. The first involved approaching at a high altitude, well above any reasonable height that would be expected. When over the airfield you then entered a spin which made it impossible to read the registration numbers, the idea being that the plane recovered from the spin just in time to make its final approach and land. This method of arrival was soon banned for not only might it lead to infringement of an overlying airway but it was all too easy to misjudge the recovery from a spin. Arriving vertically into the middle of an airfield and finding oneself sitting at the bottom of a smoking crater was not the best way subsequently to enjoy a free breakfast. The second method was exactly the opposite. It involved sneaking into the field at extremely low level taking advantage of valleys, contours of hills, or any other means of escaping detection. This was also illegal, dangerous, and banned.

On my first Breakfast Patrol I set off from Panshanger in a Piper Cub in an attempt to arrive, undetected, at Biggin Hill which I now knew quite well. All went according to plan until we crossed the river and found that fog had rolled in over Biggin Hill. Above it could be seen a mass of cavorting aircraft reminiscent of a World War I movie. Sadly, a defending Tiger Moth flew into a hill with the loss of both on board. Yet another lesson in the dangers of pushing one's enjoyment too far.

Of particular interest to me was the Percival Prentice that had just come on to the civilian register. I had flown in one as a cadet. In RAF use it was employed as a trainer with two crew in the front and one, surrounded by a mass of equipment, in the rear. It was considered to be a heavy and sturdy aircraft capable of aerobatics if sufficient space were available. To many pilots it was known as the 'Cow' as it was meant to lack the control response of most of the aircraft of its era.

The civilian version was somewhat different. There were still two full-sized pilot seats but behind them was a compartment into which it was just possible to squeeze four passengers. At the rear was a small bench made into two forward facing seats. By the knees of these passengers were two single seats facing sideways. This certainly made for an intimate atmosphere that must have been the main attraction. It was certainly not particularly comfortable. The economic facts were that six people in an aircraft made sense when funds were restricted.

Neither Tiny Marshall nor Peter Chinn appeared to have changed, and I was made welcome as ever at the Surrey and Kent Flying Club. The next step was to be checked out in this new aircraft and I was assigned to Archie, a fellow student who was also earning pocket money as a part-time instructor. As we approached the Prentice I was impressed by its size. It seemed huge and its 46 ft. wingspan with its turned-up wing tips made one appreciate that it also weighed about twice as much as anything else that I had ever flown. The cockpit appeared high above the ground and on entering I was pleased to find the pilots' seats comfortable. There was a complete panel of blind flying instruments and two primitive radios but no radio navigational aids. The brakes and flaps were pneumatically controlled and it was important to make sure that there was sufficient pressure in the system before starting the engine – otherwise an unexpected sprint across the tarmac might be made until the brakes began to function. In fact it was one of the few aircraft in which the flaps were meant to be left fully down when it was parked in order to conserve pressure. It even had a windscreen wiper, something that was very seldom found on light aircraft. Altogether the machine had a reassuringly solid feel about it.

'You're going to find the take-off interesting,' said Archie.

It certainly was!

Visibility from the cockpit was surprisingly good as we taxied around the tarmac. Opening the throttle produced an anguished howl from up front but not a great deal of other activity. We trundled sedately and noisily along the runway until the tail began to lift. This produced an excellent view of the end of the runway approaching at an ever increasing speed. At long last we eased the machine into the air. With only two of us on board we had used up most of the shorter civilian runway at Biggin Hill. The rate of climb was far from impressive and it was apparent that this was not an aircraft to take into small airfields. However, once in level flight it was easily trimmed and felt stable. After a few manoeuvres I was surprised at its agility and it could be turned in a remarkably small radius. I quickly gained confidence. Once we reached a safe height Archie turned to me. 'Now show me a stall,' he commanded.

I closed the throttle and with my new found confidence held the nose somewhat higher than my normal practice with an unfamiliar aircraft. Out of the corner of my eye I could see Archie sitting impassively with his arms crossed so I raised the nose further still, yet there was no reaction from my instructor. I therefore gave the nose one final tweak by pulling the stick hard back. This last action was followed by a shudder and then a tremendous lurch as the left wing dropped, the nose pitched down and the aircraft appeared to fall vertically out of the sky. We recovered without incident although somewhat breathless.

'Why on earth didn't you warn me?' I gasped.

'Well you seemed to have matters under control and I didn't want to spoil your fun!' came the reply.

The more I flew the Prentice the more I came to like it. It was a good touring aircraft with a reasonable cruising speed, and excellent carrying capacity. It was popular with my friends too. Day excursions to coastal airfields (at least those with long runways) were made on most fine weekends.

Sandown on the Isle of Wight boasted a long grass runway. On the day we landed it was slightly damp. I had not fully appreciated the effect of the combination of a slight uphill gradient, damp grass, and a heavily loaded aircraft until I was well into my take-off run. We lifted briefly over the road that led to the club house, settled back onto the grass of the overshoot area, and had a minor encounter with the airfield hedge as we finally became airborne. My 'co-pilot' was only on his second ever flight and assumed this was normal while none of the passengers in the back appeared to have noticed anything untoward. If they did nothing was ever said and they all returned for further flights. Otherwise our trips were relatively uneventful and we began to visit the continental seaboard. To be able to spend a day abroad and return home the same evening was an irresistible attraction. There was never a shortage of passengers.

So many exciting destinations lay within our grasp and every flight had its own adventure. The vagaries of the British weather, always at its most fickle across the English Channel, kept us on our toes. After a particularly happy day on the Belgian coast we took off from Ostend and turned westwards out to sea. With the sun against us it was hard to make out any horizon and I found myself having to look at the instruments to see if I was flying level. I began to feel uncomfortable as my senses were telling me one thing and the instruments quite another. Suddenly we were in a bank of fog and all reference to the outside world was lost.

'Roll me over, in the clover,' sang my happy passengers in the rear. Up front life was not so cheerful. Engulfed by the white vapour, I was sure that we were turning to the right and instinctively started a left turn yet the instruments showed I was already turning left and any further bank might throw us into a potentially deadly spiral dive. Sweating profusely I struggled to overcome my natural sensations and believe the instruments. Following the instruments was even more difficult made worse by the knowledge that the average life expectancy of an untrained instrument pilot flying in cloud was in the region of two minutes.

'Let's do it again,' came the raucous chant from behind me, as the song approached its climax. If only they knew what was happening in the front seat they would not have been singing quite so cheerily.

In retrospect I should have levelled the wings and then climbed into the clear air above, advising the controller of my intentions, but my inexperience left me obeying the last instruction at all costs until we broke out of the fog. This was my first encounter with spatial disorientation that has claimed the lives of countless pilots. Behind me the bawdy songs had given way to peals of laughter as my passengers happily sang away the effects of their over generous lunch. If only they had known how their pilot was feeling.

The Prentice provided a means of spreading our wings still further and it was only natural that we should look for fresh challenges. Unfortunately, my plans were to receive a setback.

The beginning of the summer was marred by the death of Tony Richmond. Tony had been taking part in a flying display and was demonstrating the manoeuvrability of the Prentice. Evidently he had attempted a slow roll at extremely low level (possibly 100 ft.) and had hit the ground with his wing tip. The aircraft was completely destroyed in the crash and resultant fire. There was a suggestion that the aircraft battery had become loose while the machine was inverted but whether or not this caused the catastrophe was uncertain. The only painful fact was that my hero, teacher and friend was dead.

Like all students I regarded my instructors as superhuman. Tony would have chastised me for any aerobatics below 4,000 ft. in a Prentice yet I firmly believed that whatever impossible feat he attempted would always work out well in his hands. Tony had taught me a great deal and my sense of grief was profound. There was also the uneasy doubt that began to enter my mind. If highly experienced former test pilots could make mistakes, what about lesser mortals like ourselves? It took many hours of self examination before I flew again.

# CHAPTER 11

# Mediterranean Capers

'TONY WOULD HAVE BEEN the first to make you fly after an incident,' said Chris, one of my more sensible friends and a future consultant Ear, Nose and Throat surgeon. 'Come on, let's take the Prentice down to the south coast.'

On a sunny weekend six of us crowded into the Prentice and flew along the south coast, admiring its many inlets, harbours and beaches. The trip was a great success and the urge to fly had returned.

'Do you realise that with a range of more than 400 miles we can really travel places,' Chris continued, 'and if we divide the cost by six it won't be too expensive. Let's go somewhere unusual.'

'How about Israel?' I countered without hesitation, thinking more about a girl friend than the logistics of the trip.

'Done!' chorused my friends. 'Now let's get a group together.'

It took no time at all to assemble a group of willing travellers; planning the journey was another matter. The furthest I had ever flown was to Paris and that was in the Air Race. My total flying experience was about 80 hours and just looking at the maps was daunting.

'How about Corsica, or Italy?' I asked the group.

'We know you can get us to Israel and back, that's where we want to go,' came the reply.

I did not need a calculator to appreciate the scale of the project. The first problem was the loading of the aircraft. The two pilots' seats were comfortable but four people in the rear compartment were going to be cramped. Apart from space, there was only a limited load carrying capability. With the fuel tanks full, and six people on board with life-jackets for flying over water, we were restricted to little more than a change of underclothes and shaving equipment.

Of my companions, one had just obtained his pilot's licence, two had never been in an aircraft before, and the others had survived day trips with me in the Prentice. I suspect that none of them really appreciated what we were attempting to do. The take-off and climb performance of the Prentice restricted us to airports with long runways that were not surrounded by mountains. These airports were usually used by commercial or military aircraft requiring radio communication. Although the Prentice carried two primitive radios, each only held six crystals for preset frequencies. One crystal on each radio was used for the emergency frequency leaving us with ten frequencies for the entire trip. This complicated still further the choice of airfields we could use. We were also faced with the lack of climb performance, and the need to select a route that did not require us to climb much above 4,000 ft. Planning the route took far longer than expected. We also had to obtain permission from the Israeli authorities in case we ever managed to reach their air space.

The Surrey and Kent Flying Club gave us every encouragement and took the Prentice over to Gatwick for us. This saved us the problem of an intermediate landing to clear customs as this could be carried out at Gatwick. It also spared us the worries of a take-off from Biggin Hill at full weight.

On 15 July 1960, G-AOLR was fully laden with six excited students. Full of enthusiasm and hope we loaded our aircraft with fuel, safety equipment, charts and minimal luggage. In the rear the passengers sat, knee to knee, surrounded by maps and pieces of luggage. I had some 80 hours experience in my logbook and we were ready to go.

The first leg of our journey was planned from Gatwick to Lyon, by far the longest non-stop flight I had ever made. The aircraft had no radio navigation aid, and we were going to have to rely on map-reading. A cool breeze blew down Gatwick's long runway which assisted our westerly take-off and then we turned south-east. The start was very encouraging as we crossed the English coast on track at Beachy Head. Drift and ground speed had been calculated on a vintage Dalton 'computer,' a circular calculating device that has assisted more than one generation of aviators. The passengers in the rear sat, knees interlocked, acting as assistant navigators. They were delighted when we made landfall on the French coast at Dieppe some 40 minutes later, on track and on time. Our landfall was duly noted in the log. This was going to be a piece of cake!

I maintained a steady heading across north-western France and after some thirty minutes we caught sight of the River Seine with its characteristic 'S' bends to the west of Paris. The Prentice droned serenely across the changing landscape. With Paris behind we were entering unfamiliar territory. Villages and roads abounded, identification was the main problem. Behind me I was aware that my assistant navigators were craning their necks and discussing our possible whereabouts.

I reassured myself. We had noted the time we had crossed the Seine, and I had flown a constant heading since then at a steady speed. The area of uncertainty must be small.

A map contains an amazing amount of information. Hills, contours of valleys, and the entire geography of the region are distilled into this piece of paper. If you can read a map all the beauty of the scenery is there in your hands. But it is also a contract. The terms are simple. If you start at one point on the map and proceed across it in a given direction it shows the country you will cross and the topography of your destination. But what if you broke the contract? Suppose you marked the wrong starting point, what if the wind had changed direction and strength? Had we marked the wrong 'S' bend on the Seine? All these doubts began to assail me as we droned on.

Behind me, the assistant navigators had anxious expressions as we all looked for landmarks. Then I spied the town. According to the time we had flown and my heading that had not changed, it should have been Auxerre. The pattern of railway lines looked correct. As Captain I should have had the confidence to enter it into the Navigation Log and to have continued. The problem was that no one else agreed with me. They claimed that it was Montargis, which had a similar pattern of railway lines but this would have placed us way off track. Before proceeding further into the unknown it was obviously important to remove any doubt.

'Can you pinpoint our position?' Chris called.

I recalled my Tiger Moth days and explained my plan of action. Before long we were down to tree top level and howling along the railway line towards the unsuspecting town ahead. The first thing that became obvious was that flying a heavily loaded Prentice at low level was a far cry from the feather-light, highly manoeuvrable Tiger Moth. Judging by the upturned faces we were obviously making a great deal of noise.

'Station ahead!' called John.

The next chain of events appeared to happen instantaneously. I recall a mass of white upturned faces on the platform followed by:

'Auxerre!' shouted Phil.

'Maniac!' yelled Chris.

'Look out!' cried John.

I looked out in time to see a gargoyle on the side of Auxerre Cathedral approaching our starboard wing with some rapidity. A hasty left turn and we began our slow and laborious climb back to 4,000 ft. which was our normal cruising altitude. We had at least confirmed our position and I had learnt yet another lesson. Ahead was the high ground of the Massif Central that would require every scrap of altitude that we could coax out of our machine.

As we proceeded south-east, helped by a following wind, the countryside became more hilly. There was an abundance of landmarks and the Prentice cruised comfortably above the green hills, sunlit villages, and narrow valleys. The hills fell away two hours later and we caught our first sight of Lyon. There could be no mistaking this city. Apart from its size the confluence of the rivers Saône and Rhône in the city's centre could be seen from a surprising distance. The airport of Bron lay to the east and we made an uneventful approach. We spent the evening in Lyon, our only mistake having been to enquire from an enthusiastic taxi driver about the performance of his new Citroen station wagon. This vehicle

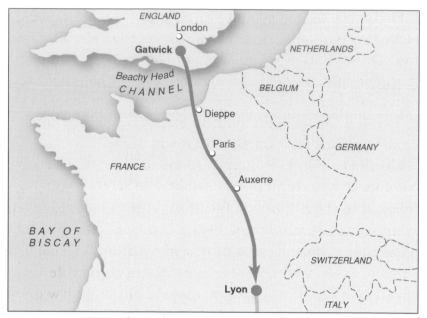

*Our planned route from Gatwick to Lyon.*

moved surprisingly quickly and, as he was proud to point out, its novel air suspension allowed it to be driven over kerbs with no apparent ill effect.

Our plan for the next day was to fly to Nice. The direct track over high mountains was out of the question for the Prentice. We devised two alternatives: the less demanding followed the Rhône Valley down to Marseille and then followed the coastline to Nice, an extremely lengthy journey. A variation was to follow the Rhône southwards as far as Avignon and there turn south-east looking for valleys through the Alps Maritime until we reached the coast to the east of Toulon where we would turn east along the coast to Nice. This was shorter than flying down to Marseille and was our preferred route.

Departing from Lyon in the morning we very quickly picked up the Rhône and followed it southwards. This was fun. On the left the jagged mountains projected into the morning light, on the right were hills, all we had to do was to follow the meandering river identifying each town as we progressed. We gave the military air base at Orange a wide berth as we had been warned that it was active.

North of Avignon we turned to the south-east leaving the comforting river behind. We had little difficulty finding the valley of the river Durance but as we began to approach the mountains it became hazy. Flying in mountainous terrain requires special techniques particularly in an under-powered aircraft. Every now and then some strange invisible force would kick the aircraft so that it would pitch and jaw quite violently. Then we would find ourselves descending followed by a bump as we were thrown upwards. There was one stage when we simply continued descending despite the application of full throttle. Only then did my earlier gliding training come back and I turned away from the descending air to look for an up-draught on the other side of the valley.

'Pass the sick bag,' called Phil, who had gone a pale shade of green.

Fortunately nobody used them as we bucked our way through the valleys. Up front I struggled to ensure we remained on course and clear of the rocky high ground.

'There's the sea,' shouted John.

I followed his outstretched hand and, sure enough, there was a deep blue patch on the horizon. We all cheered up as the patch grew in size to provide us with our first glimpse of the Mediterranean. The tension and the turbulence subsided as we crossed the coast. Small matter that we were off

course; we quickly identified our position and followed the
spectacular coastline eastwards. By the time we landed at
Nice our confidence and colour were back to normal.

The next leg to Corsica involved a long sea crossing of
well over an hour. This was by far the longest that I had ever
attempted. Our landfall was to be on the northern tip of
Corsica, but we knew that the island was famous not only
for its bandits but for the high mountains that covered most
of it. We certainly did not wish to blunder into them if they
were hidden in cloud; neither did we wish to miss the
northern tip of the island even though we had sufficient fuel
to reach the Italian coastline.

Our destination, Bastia, lay on the island's east coast and
so the plan was to cross the northern tip and then turn south
following the coast. I was particularly careful to calculate
drift before we left Nice. The first part of the crossing was
made in good weather but ahead the sky had taken on a deep
blue hue. As we flew on the dark blue turned to black. Those
in the rear might not have noticed the darkening sky, but
they were certainly aware of the changing sea. The calm blue
had long given way to rolling waves and now angry white
flecks could be seen on them like fingers reaching up into
the wind. A complete wall of blackness lay ahead as the
torrential rain poured from a storm raging over northern
Corsica. I turned eastwards while we consulted the maps. We
had sufficient fuel to reach Italy and we could have retraced
our steps, but first I elected to see if we could fly around the
storm and still reach Bastia. Only static and odd screeches
could be heard on the radio. Keeping a respectable distance
from the storm we skirted Corsica until we were well to the
east and then turned south.

'It's clear,' shouted Phil, who was the first to notice that Bastia was clear of any significant weather.

When we landed there it was hard to imagine the severe weather that was battering the island ten miles to the north – unless you looked at the clouds. A delightful taxi driver befriended us. Once he had established that it was not his friend's sisters we sought but simply straightforward accommodation he drove us at breakneck speed over the mountainous roads to show us his island of which he was so proud. Our new friend found us good food and clean accommodation and arranged to meet us in the morning. Our return trip to the airport would have impressed a professional rally driver.

'Do you realise,' mused Chris, 'the most dangerous part of the trip so far has been the taxi rides.'

Later that day he had reason to change his mind.

We took off next day in the pale blue morning sky and beautiful crystal clear air. Puffs of cumulus drifted past, almost lazily, and we were soon admiring the legendary island of Monte Cristo that projected out of the water like a cardboard cut-out. We set course for the Italian mainland. Our navigational exercises could not have been simpler. Once the Italian coastline was reached at Cittavechia we were to follow it south-eastwards passing west of Rome, over the islands of Ponza until we reached Naples, our refuelling stop. The details of the Italian coastline were lost in the haze but we flew directly over the islands of Ponza which looked like a collection of flattened marbles on an azure floor. The island of Ischia appeared like a sandcastle floating on water but with a peak of 2,500 ft. Then we turned east into Naples Bay. The airport at Naples was hidden in the shimmering haze that covered the entire Naples Bay area. I knew where the airport must be but still I could not see it. Then I spotted it.

'Lima Romeo cleared to land,' crackled the controller's voice.

'The airport's on top of the hill,' I pointed out to those in the rear. I reached for the flap lever.

'Break left, break left for Christ sake!' screamed Chris.

I didn't hesitate to ask what had prompted this outburst from the normally sanguine Chris. I broke left as sharply as I dared as a military jet with American markings, like some ugly predator, cruised past making for the same runway. We watched as the Phantom landed in a puff of burnt rubber but not a word from the controller.

'Naples Tower, I've just had to avoid a Phantom on finals.'

'Lima Romeo, you are cleared to land,' came the unconcerned reply.

We later found out that a military controller operating on a separate frequency had given the Phantom permission to land without checking with his civilian counterpart.

Naples was hot, burning hot. The tarmac looked wet in the heat. The Air Traffic Control Office, the Customs Office, and the Meteorological Office appeared to be miles apart so that obtaining clearances was an exhausting process. Each office required forms to be stamped, while obtaining fuel seemed to take for ever. We were dripping with perspiration by the time these tasks had been completed.

The aircraft was baking hot. The metal structures burnt our skin so that climbing on board required a great deal of care. We kept the hatches open as we taxied out. I was somewhat apprehensive about the next leg which was one of the most difficult for it meant crossing the Apennines, a range of mountains that runs the length of Italy. Our destination was Brindisi, and there was no hope that we could climb over the mountains. However, there was a valley that ran north-east from Naples to Benevento at which point we could turn south-east towards the port of Bari and from there on towards Brindisi. The main point was not to get lost.

Freely perspiring I began the take-off run. If I had fully understood the devastating effect of heat on aircraft performance I would have perspired even more freely. I had never heard of the term 'density altitude', let alone understood its significance. We seemed to use up a great deal of Naples' enormously long runway before the rumble of the wheels ceased. We crossed the airfield boundary at about 50 ft. and the aircraft refused to climb any more. Fortunately Naples airport is on top of a hill and all I could do was to hold the aircraft in the air. There is a limit to how far forward I could push the throttle. I could not only see the details of the windows and doors of individual buildings but could identify individual garments hanging on the washing lines. Why do people in hot climates wear so many black clothes, I wondered. However, my thoughts snapped back to more immediate concerns, I was extremely low, and there was nothing else I could do. All six cylinders of the Gipsy Queen engine howled their protest at being held continuously at full throttle but those in the back were having a marvellous time. They assumed that I had laid on this low level roof skimming sector for the benefit of their photography.

'Drop the left wing,' called Phil, camera poised.

I didn't reply as I was more worried about dropping the entire aircraft!

Gradually the city fell behind us as we headed out into the

bay. Somehow we had managed to climb about 300 ft. but now, at least, the altimeter showed some sign of movement in the right direction. Ahead lay the Island of Capri like some beautifully decorated plum pudding. On our left Mount Vesuvius brooded over the entire region. Slowly, unbelievably slowly, the altimeter showed us gaining height but it took nearly thirty minutes before we gained sufficient altitude to turn back over the city of Naples and begin our passage through the valleys.

A knife-edged hilly ridge lay ahead across our path and the turbulence began. The Prentice bucked and twisted, the heat haze limited visibility but we found our way along the valley with its patchwork of brown grass fields, stone walls and white villages. Despite being thrown around we were able to identify the monastery, the town of Benevento, and then a small lake as we changed our heading to the south-east. For more than an hour we droned on across the narrow spine of Italy until we began to realise that the hills were less menacing and the countryside was beginning to flatten. It all looked burnt from the sun.

'There's Bari,' called John, pointing to a sizeable whitish blur on the horizon in our 11 o'clock. We flew on for some time before we saw the Adriatic. Bari slid past our left wing as we obliquely joined the coast. Brindisi airport was just to the north of the port and we were surprisingly close before we were able to make radio contact.

Brindisi was a shared military and civil facility. We were greeted warmly by the staff in the civil terminal. Armed guards seemed to be everywhere. A small, rotund and rather pompous man arrived. 'I am the Airport Manager,' he said, 'and this airport is very important.'

*Our path from Lyon to Nice, Nice to Bastia, Bastia to Naples
and from Naples to Brindisi.*

He twiddled with his moustache. 'Albania is a hostile nation and we are the closest airfield to it. We must always be in a constant state of readiness. Always keep your passports with you and make sure your documents are correctly stamped in my office.'

He then proceeded to stamp every piece of paper at least twice.

'I must formally warn you that if you stray into Albanian air space you will be fired on.'

I imagine he meant by the Albanians but the words came out with such venom that we just wondered. On that note he spun around and left the room. The rest of the staff, and the guards, were friendly and helpful, and advised us what to see in Brindisi. So strict was the security that the guards failed to notice some of us slept in the aircraft to save money.

At 04.30 a.m. next morning Anglo-Italian relationships reached their lowest ebb. The carnet, which at that time was like the International Passport of the aircraft, could not be found. I remembered the stamping ceremony of the previous day.

'It must be locked in the Manager's office,' I told the Duty Manager.

'I don't have the keys, do you really want me to wake him and bring him to the airport?'

'I'm sorry, we can't go without it,' I replied.

Any semblance of ill humour the Aerodrome Manager might have shown the day before paled into insignificance compared with his features in the morning. He unlocked the office with a surly grunt and began a search. After ten minutes he invited his staff to help look but to no avail. This seemed the end of the trip for without the carnet there was nowhere we could go. Shortly afterwards Phil came into the ransacked office wearing a happy satisfied smile.

'Look what I found under the rear seats,' he grinned, waving the carnet above his head.

My relief was short-lived. The Airport Manager's eyes bulged in their sockets and he made a strange gobbling sound, then he exploded. None of us realised that Italian (or any other language for that matter) could be spoken so loudly, so quickly, and for such a length of time. We did not understand the words but the inference was very clear. With ears ringing and tails between our legs we departed Brindisi and followed the coastline to the south-east before setting out over the Adriatic. We calculated when we had entered Greek air space, at least we hoped it was Greek, and continued scanning the haze looking for our first landfall. A cheer went up as we crossed a small island to the north-west of Corfu that meant that we were well clear of Albania and directly on track. Radio contact was impossible, but once we were over the island of Corfu we were able to make some exchanges. From the air the island looked remarkably green and abounding with golden beaches. Its beauty was enhanced by marking the end of a worrying sector.

We flew on southwards, following the mountainous Greek shore. The mountains seemed to march down into the sea and the coastline was studded with numerous bays and inlets. The air base at Preveza guarded the entrance to an enormous bay. It was certainly strategically placed but with water all around it any landing or take-off mishaps were going to result in a ducking. Ahead, a large mountainous finger projected westwards. This was the island of Levkas but there was a narrow passage between it and the mainland through which we flew. Small islands were scattered offshore but there seemed to be a complete absence of people. Occasionally we spotted isolated groups of buildings or small towns. It seemed inconceivable that such a beautiful part of Europe should be so deserted. Far on the right we spotted the airfield of Araxos which had agreed to our refuelling there. The runway looked vast, but there was no sign of buildings, aircraft, or any human activity. The only evidence of habitation was the crackling of the controller's voice in our head-sets who confirmed our permission to land and the availability of fuel. The runway was pristine with no sign of any rubber marks, as if it were a ghost field. We landed and the distant voice gave us taxiing instructions to a remote piece of concrete. Then we were told to switch off and wait. The heat was intense but the silence was eerie. Nothing stirred apart from a northerly breeze. We stretched our legs, stayed near the aircraft and waited. Then we noticed a cloud of dust. A small white van emerged from this cloud with two officials who brought us drinks and sandwiches. The tanker appeared out of nowhere, the tanks were filled and we were politely but firmly ushered on our way. When we landed on the hot runway I felt certain that we had left some rubber marks on it. When we came to take-off the runway was gleaming spotless.

The generous length of runway and the steady breeze helped our take-off run and we were soon cruising along the southern shore of the Gulf of Corinth. Patras, one of Greece's larger cities, passed by on the right. The occasional ship left its clearly defined wake and the mountains either side reached heavenwards; this was majestic scenery. It was also a period for relaxation and enjoyment. At the eastern end of the gulf we looked for the Corinth Canal, that masterpiece of engineering. The canal was so narrow and the sides so steep that we could not make out the water until we were directly overhead. We orbited more than once to allow the photographers to get their shots.

We continued east with Athens in a haze off our port wing. We set course for Rhodes, a sector of the flight that took us from island to island. Each one was more beautiful than the next; some had hidden harbours, others appeared to have no population but all were surrounded by an indigo coloured sea with a bright blue band near the shore. It looked as though some giant had thrown down pieces of a jigsaw puzzle, each with its own mountain and each with a golden border. For a while we skirted the mountainous southern coast of Turkey.

'Aircraft at 10 o'clock!' shouted John.

I couldn't make it out. It was at about our height but the size and distance were difficult to judge. Then we realised it was a large bird, possibly an eagle. It turned away as we approached. Then we caught sight of Rhodes, with its northern tip pointing like a finger at the Turkish coastline. Like the other island it had its own private mountains, its golden beaches, and spectacular coastline, but it was larger. The ancient harbour, home of one of the seven wonders of the world, the Colossus, sat next to a newer port crammed with boats. The airport, Maritsa, looked rather close to a mountain although the main runway was well clear of any high ground. The island appeared to have its own private cooling breeze and at ground level the beaches appeared even more inviting than they did from the air. We unanimously decided to spend a day exploring the island. A day was not enough, but it was all we could spare. The island was steeped in history. Invaders such as the Knights of St. John and, more recently, the Italians have left their marks on the architecture of the city. No one could spoil the natural beauty.

Take-off we knew was going to pose a problem. Rhodes now has a new airport but in those days the airfield Maritsa had one long runway that faced the prevailing wind, though the last half of it had a marked uphill slope. There was a

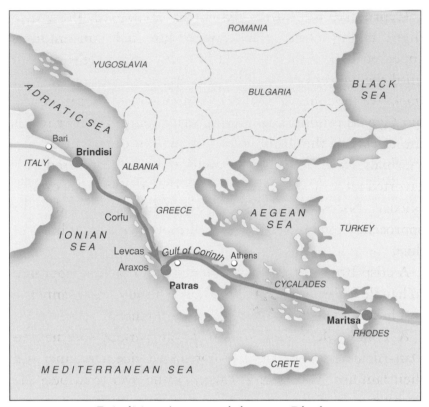

*Brindisi to Araxos and thence to Rhodes.*

shorter cross runway close to the mountain suitable only for a lightly laden Spitfire. The uphill slope worried me. There was only one thing to do. We walked the length of the runway to assess the terrain beyond. A valley ran down to the beach some three miles away. With sadness we loaded the aircraft, said goodbye to the friends we had made and started up. In the cool of the morning and a steady breeze along the runway the take-off was uneventful. We spent some ten minutes to the west of the island gaining altitude before we dared to turn eastwards across it.

Cyprus lay more than two hours away with the entire flight taking place over water. Our fuel consumption appeared higher than normal but we saw no sight of land until the western coast of Cyprus appeared more or less on track. We thought we had become accustomed to turbulence, but Cyprus produced its own special variety. Whether it was the effects of the Troudos mountains on our right or just thermals from the heat we neither knew nor cared. We cavorted rather than flew across the island towards its capital, Nicosia. Nicosia lay in a shimmering dusty haze, and as we approached the entire area seemed more like a giant bowl of dust.

A crisp British voice answered our radio call and appeared to handle its busy traffic in an efficient almost curt manner.

'Lima Romeo cleared to land,' he announced.

A 'Follow Me' vehicle took us to our parking spot next to Dan-Air who were busy transporting service personnel and their families. Two of their aircrew came over to inspect the Prentice.

'How did you get here from England in that?' they gasped. I explained our route to them.

'Well if you must fly further, Beirut is nearer and it's less water to cross. If you really want to go to Israel once you've put in your flight plan you either land there, back here, or in the water. Do not even think of diverting to a neighbouring country. If you have to ditch the RAF has a base at Akrotiri with good rescue facilities – but *don't divert*. Good luck!' they smiled and sauntered back to their aircraft.

Of course, we were excited at the prospect of completing the final leg. By now we were experienced navigators, the weather was good, and Nicosia both helpful and efficient. I

*Phil recovering from our emergency landing in Nicosia.*

still do not know which of these factors was to blame but the fact is that I refuelled, flight planned, and took off in the midday heat. Within two minutes we were in serious trouble as the aircraft refused to climb. I thought of forced landing in the ravine that trapped us but our high ground speed and the large unfriendly boulders combined to dissuade me. Desperately I looked for rising air. There was obviously no way in which a heavily laden Prentice could be turned within a thermal like a sail plane, but we did gain 500 ft. which we then lost in about 45 seconds. I must have bent the throttle linkage trying to coax more power out of the engine. It took about 25 minutes to reach 1,000 ft. and I could manoeuvre the aircraft. The engine was overheating but the passengers were in an even worse state.

No one cared about turbulence, all we wanted to do was to land. The controller was aware of our problem and when

I called, 'Lima Romeo has now reached 1,000 ft. returning to land,' I was greeted with, 'Congratulations, Lima Romeo cleared to land.'

My log book shows a flight of 55 minutes but we all aged several years. The ever friendly crew of the Dan Air York parked next to us took one look at our faces and rushed over with refreshments. They even lent us more modern safety equipment and advised us where to go for the rest of the day. We left the aircraft and departed for the 'Five Mile' beach at Kyrenia which was a welcome relief.

Next morning we planned for an early departure. This time it was Air Traffic who warned us again about not diverting to a neighbouring country.

'You must land in Israel, back here or in the water,' the officer said without a smile as he stamped the flight plan.

'Watch your navigation,' he said, but this time with a smile.

We almost soared into the cool morning air and climbed for our two hour flight to Tel Aviv. Between Nicosia and the south-east of Cyprus we checked our drift very carefully before setting out over the Eastern Mediterranean. We soon lost radio contact with Nicosia, and as the island disappeared behind into the haze we had only the compass and the beat of the engine to maintain our interest.

As the coastline of Cyprus receded into the haze we were alone once again. No radio contact, just the occasional ship. Eyes glued to the compass, we maintained our heading while listening to every beat of the engine. The warnings about not straying into neighbouring airspace were still fresh in our ears. After about an hour and a half we thought we could see a coastline, or was it cloud?

'There are hills on the coast,' called John.

'Fathead!' shouted Chris, waving the map. 'The coast is flat around Tel Aviv.'

We were flying almost directly into the sun, but there was no mistaking the hills. The map showed all too clearly that the only hilly coastline was near Beirut, miles into Lebanon. It was impossible we could be so far off course on a relatively short leg – or was it? Feeling somewhat nervous, I maintained our heading. After an anxious four minutes we were able to raise Tel Aviv on the radio. We were on track. The explanation for the hills was simple. The coastline was covered by patchy low cloud and the hills we could see were, in fact, well inland on the road to Jerusalem.

We descended over the old port of Jaffa and out of the haze emerged Lydda airport as it was then called. Judging by our reception we might have just flown the Atlantic. We were warmly greeted and a pretty girl came to make us a presentation. There seemed to be a general consensus that we were more than slightly eccentric, possibly even mad to have made the journey in such an aircraft. The local maintenance organisation fell over themselves to be accommodating. The poor Prentice had suffered on the journey, but there were no engine problems.

Naturally we wanted to fly around the country but we were advised of the security complications. Ten times over we were warned how small the country was and how easy it was to stray across a border and to be fired upon. Everyone seemed interested in the Prentice. Outside the maintenance hangar sat a Mustang; it seemed huge. The giant four-bladed propeller overshadowed the entrance to the hangar. Its camouflage paintwork was covered by generous deposits

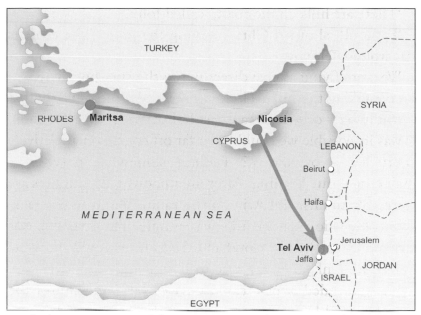

*Rhodes to Nicosia and from Nicosia to Tel Aviv. (Borders as they existed in 1960.)*

of dust as it sat, squat like some prehistoric monster. Indentations on the leading edges of the wings looked like the result of wire strikes.

'Why don't you climb into the cockpit?' my host asked.

It seemed a long way up and it was baking hot, but I felt a strange thrill simply to sit in this powerful machine. Most of the instruments were familiar although the airspeed was calibrated in miles per hour rather than knots. I puzzled over a warning notice about exceeding a high indicated airspeed at high altitude – surely the machine could not enter the transonic zone? In any case, judging by the wire strikes it looked as though it had been flown at the lower extreme of the altitude range. The most impressive and frightening feature was that I could not see anything forward apart from the vast extent of the engine cowling stretching away ahead. My host read my thoughts:

'Don't worry, you can see fine when the tail comes up.' I had my doubts.

'It needs a bootful of rudder on take-off but it's a real thoroughbred. You won't find a better tank buster,' he continued. 'Would you like to fly it?'

I suppose I must have nodded my head before I wondered if I was really capable of controlling this 7-ton monster. In retrospect he was probably teasing me just to see my reaction to his offer. However, he took it a stage further.

'OK, climb out, we'll go and see the boss, get you briefed and kitted out.' His use of English suddenly gave away that he must have served in the RAF. The boss was also friendly but spoke English with an accent. He listened attentively while my host spoke in Hebrew, but I could see from the reddening of his scarred neck, the downturn of the mouth, and the waving of his hand that he was unimpressed, very unimpressed.

'My friend,' he half-smiled, 'we have every confidence in your flying skills but it is quite impossible for a foreign civilian to fly a military aircraft. Any flying in our country will have to be in your machine, and I will be pleased to help you obtain the clearances.'

I expressed understanding and disappointment but I was secretly relieved. It was to be another thirty years before I actually flew a Mustang. True to his word, we were cleared to make two local flights. Flying north towards Haifa we were amazed at the narrowness of the country. In the Mustang I could have been across the border while still

*Inverted in a Mustang some 30 years later.*

struggling with the undercarriage. The heat haze made for poor visibility and gave the impression of flying in a goldfish bowl. The southern flight took us along the coast towards Ashkelon.

# CHAPTER 12

# Back to London

WE DIVIDED UP to visit different parts of the country and Chris managed to get second degree burns from the sun. All too soon the time for our return approached. The two short flights in Israel had posed no problem for the Prentice with four people on board and with minimal fuel. The pilot, on the other hand, had to be constantly aware of his position, as even the pedestrian cruising speed of the Prentice could carry it across borders very easily.

Since we intended to fly two or three legs on the first day of our return trip we elected for a dawn take-off. This would allow us to land and depart from Nicosia well before the temperature reached its peak. To be absolutely sure of an early take-off, the flight plan was put in the night before and four of us slept at the airport. 0500 hrs has never been the best hour of my life, but the pleasant air traffic controller made it worse.

'I'm sorry, you will have to delay your departure at least four hours as there are military exercises and the airspace on your route is closed to civil traffic.'

'But why on earth didn't you tell us yesterday?' I gasped.

'Does a four hour delay really matter on a journey of your length?' he countered.

I explained the problem, pointing out that if we arrived in Nicosia during the heat of the day we could not take off again.

'I'll tell you what I'll do, I'll phone the Chief of the Air Force and ask him to authorise transit of the exercise area,' he smiled.

Startled, I watched him dial and listened as he spoke in Hebrew to several people.

'Ezer...' he began. Although I could not understand the conversation it was obvious that he was addressing the Chief of the Air Force by his first name. He put the phone down and grinned.

'Your flight is authorised and the Chief of the Air Force wishes you a pleasant trip.'

As we taxied towards runway 29 the sky was no longer black in the east. The glow behind us was increasing surprisingly quickly. The sky brightened even more rapidly as we climbed on a north-west heading, now with the coast behind us. We could only admire the crimson and orange tinges of the scattered cumulus as we laboured upwards. It was so strange to be bathed in sunlight while beneath us the earth was still shrouded in darkness. It was yet another facet to the magic of flight.

The reverie was shattered as a speck on the surface of one pinkish cloud rapidly grew into the shape of an approaching aircraft. Within moments we identified it as a Meteor and it was towing a target. Where was the rest of the squadron? We didn't wait to find out but turned away and dived into a patch of clear air. Shortly afterwards we bade farewell to the Israel controller and began the long over-water trek against the wind towards Cyprus.

'Coast ahead,' called John who had the eagle eyes.

We crossed the coast of Cyprus exactly on track near Larnaca and bounced our way across the hinterland towards

Nicosia. Although it was warm, it was still far from hot as we hurried through the formalities, refuelled and took-off – without incident. Retracing our route westwards across Cyprus and then out into the Mediterranean seemed almost routine. Of course, it did not prevent us listening to the beat of the engine and scanning the gauges but we were a very different team from the group who flew the outbound journey.

'Rhodes ahead,' called John, as the island appeared on the horizon exactly on time, about two hours later. On the right the mountainous and indented coastline of Turkey could be made out.

Rhodes had lost none of its attraction but we had no time to spare. A blissful 20 knot wind was blowing along the runway and the temperature was only moderately hot. I reckoned we should have no problem with the take-off. True to form we lumbered into the air to begin the stunning island hopping sector that would eventually take us to Athens. Even my hardy crew were surprised by the turbulence over the land as we approached Athens.

Invisible rushes of rising air threw us from side to side making the aircraft difficult to steady. Ahead Athens lay in a great bowl within a semi-circle of hills. A pall of dust or haze hung over the city. The airfield was next to the sea but the haze made it difficult to distinguish landmarks. We could almost see the heat.

'Feels like a Turkish bath,' called John from the back.

Descriptive as it might be the remark was totally inappropriate for a landing in Athens of all places. As we switched off the heat hit us on the breezeless airfield. We were not going any further. Fortunately, the beach was close by and I thought we had earned some blissful refreshment. It was obviously going to require an early morning departure on the next day. Two of the group elected to spend more time in Athens and make their way home by train. Chris, who had been doing sterling work in the back with the maps, was promoted to co-pilot.

Airfields in the predawn hours are exciting places. Unlit and brooding, shadowy forms of parked aircraft can be made out against the background of blue taxiway lights. The heat of the day has long since vanished so that the air is cool, slightly damp in fact, and a faint layer of mist might be found a few feet above the ground. The excitement is that a new day is not far off and that you are about to witness its birth while airborne. We checked the aircraft, taxied out and began our take-off as the first fingers of light penetrated the sky behind us. The Prentice relished the cool air and with just four aboard soared into the sky.

'Look at that!' shouted Chris, as the orange light struck the Acropolis on our right. We were obliged to turn left and out to sea towards Corinth. Our engine seemed bent on hammering away at the silence of the dawn for nothing else was moving. In the rear, John and Phil, now with the luxury of being able to stretch their legs, had no trouble identifying landmarks. The Corinth Canal was spotted and photographed once again and we followed the spectacular curved passage along the Gulf of Corinth. We happily picked out familiar landmarks passing well to the north of Araxos before we altered our heading northwards to Corfu. It all seemed so straightforward and Chris was comfortable in his new role.

Corfu was just as beautiful as it had been on the outbound

leg. We bade farewell to Greece and set off across the Aegean Sea for the Italian coastline.

'At least there's no danger of flying into Albania going this way,' said Phil reassuringly.

We planned to reach the Italian coastline about 30 miles south-east of Brindisi. The low-lying coast appeared on schedule and we seemed to be on track.

'I'll try and raise Brindisi on the radio,' I called.

Much to my surprise my call received an immediate response. There was a burst of static, a few screeches, and then I thought I heard a controller say, 'Lima Romeo, you are 30 miles south-east of Brindisi.'

'That's pretty good,' I smiled at Chris. 'I didn't think the Italians had such an efficient radar service.'

Instead of smiling back at me Chris looked horrorstruck; his eyes and mouth were open but no sound emanated.

I saw the tracers before the aircraft. Three Sabre jets, elegant with their swept wings, swooped past our starboard wing, guns blazing at some unseen target. Ahead of us a streak of flame marked the passage of a rocket. Chris regained his powers of speech.

'Get out of here for Christ's sake,' he said. 'There is an air firing zone 30 miles south-east of Brindisi.'

I had already turned left ninety degrees and was getting out of the area as fast as we could travel. It took a little while for us to calm down.

'Harold,' called Phil. 'Have you thought of the reception we might have at Brindisi?'

'Wasn't that one bad enough?'

'It wasn't the rockets I was thinking of,' Phil continued, 'It's the Airport Manager.'

With all the events of the trip I had completely forgotten our early morning debacle on the outbound journey. Still, there was nowhere else to go with a safe fuel reserve.

'Welcome back,' smiled the Duty Manager. 'The Aerodrome Manager is on holiday so I'll be looking after you. Just make sure you don't lose your carnet!'

The news from the Met. Office was not so good. A line of thunderstorms stretched across the mountains blocking our route. There was nothing else to do apart from spending the night in Brindisi, and to hope that the storms would clear by the next day. We went back to collect our kit from the aircraft to find a small group of Americans examining the Prentice with curiosity. Next to us was parked a twin-engine Beechcraft with US military markings.

'How far have you flown in this?'

I explained the journey so far.

'Jeesus!' was the only reply.

'Where are you off to?' I politely enquired.

'Naples.'

'What about the storms?'

'Oh, we'll get around them in this aircraft,' the pilot smiled, pointing at the twin fins.

We were still in the terminal when a group of ashen-faced individuals staggered in through the swing doors. It took a moment or two for us to recognise them as the party who had set off with such confidence less than an hour before.

'Buddy, you made the right decision,' grinned one of the pilots.

The next day was bright and clear without a trace of cloud in the sky. We climbed away in the fresh morning air and were soon able to make out Bari on our right. Somehow the navigation seemed so routine, giving us time to admire the mountains of central Italy. The turn at Benevento, and the passage through the valleys, all passed without incident. We made contact with Naples.

'Lima Romeo cleared to land,' came the response.

'I'm not taking any chances,' called Chris looking all round the horizon.

'Seems clear,' called Phil and John, and so we landed back at Naples. It was hot, but we had come to expect it. Moreover, we knew our way around the airfield so that by dividing up the tasks we were able to refuel, clear customs and flight plan remarkably quickly.

'Are we going to be all right for take-off?' Chris enquired anxiously.

Evidently he had not forgotten our roof hopping exploits.

'Judging by the performance so far we should be fine,' I replied, and opened the throttle. We left the ground after a relatively short run.

'Gee, what a difference!' exclaimed Chris.

We actually climbed out over the bay! From then on it was a simple run following the coastline past Rome with the engine running sweetly. Almost routine in fact. This time we picked out both the islands of Monte Cristo and Pianosa before landing at Bastia for refuelling. With Bastia behind us John and Phil in the back were able to admire the mountainous spine of Corsica which we could see clearly for the first time. I followed the coast northwards. From the lighthouse on the northern tip of Corsica we set course for Nice. The Mediterranean looked calm and inviting. This stretch of water that had worried us so much on the outbound leg now seemed but a minor obstacle.

'Coast ahead,' called John.

Sure enough the mainland coast was emerging out of the haze. We were exactly on track and landed at Nice without delay. It seemed a good idea to spend the night there before facing the mountains.

The sky looked inviting as we checked our charts before take-off.

'Are we in for a rough ride?' asked Phil.

'I don't think so, the wind is not too strong and the temperature hasn't built up.'

'The exit route looks a trifle complex,' complained Chris, thumbing the charts.

'Not for experienced pilots like us!' I grinned.

I was right. We had no trouble identifying the route, flying through the valleys towards the Rhône. Nobody even commented on the occasional bump. Some two and a half hours later we landed in Lyon.

'Chris, organise the refuelling, I'll go and check the weather,' I called.

The weather ahead was dreadful. There was an active front across our path with low cloud and heavy rain.

'Try tomorrow, it should be much better,' the Met Officer smiled.

It seemed like sensible advice. The forecast next morning was indeed much better. There was a front across our route but clearing rapidly to the east. By the time we took off the weather should be fine en route. On the morning of our fifth day we left Lyon bound for Gatwick. Half an hour after departure I noted that the sky was overcast but thought nothing of it as I was so intent on accurate navigation. The overcast gradually lowered but the danger signs of an approaching front were completely lost on me as I made the occasional correction for drift.

'Bits of lowish cloud,' Chris muttered from the right-hand seat.

'Must be isolated,' I replied. 'The forecast was good.'

By now it was raining but not very heavily and still we maintained our heading. I was fascinated by the water that built up on the edge of the windscreen, and turned on the windscreen wiper. With a hiss and screech the blade rushed back and forth across the windscreen, not that it made any difference as we were in cloud and I still could not see anything.

'How much more of this stuff?' enquired Chris.

'Can't be much or we would have been warned about it.'

I was wrong. We were now flying in solid cloud and I was concentrating on the artificial horizon and heading indicator, perspiring freely, and knowing that I had to trust the instruments and overcome my natural sensations. If anything the weather was getting worse and we had been flying for more than an hour without a navigational fix.

'What are we going to do?' Chris asked in a strangely calm voice.

'We're certainly not going to descend blind over the hills. At the worst we'll have to fly on our present heading for another 90 minutes and then descend when we should be over the Channel.'

'Where do you reckon we are?'

Chris pointed about 50 miles south-west of Paris.

'Let's see if we can get some help.'

None of our radio calls received any response. Occasionally we saw the odd patch of ground, and once even a railway line, but I had at last learnt to resist the siren-like attraction of descending into what might be a valley surrounded by unseen hills. The windscreen wiper had given up the unequal struggle. The blade was now rotating uselessly around its arm so I switched it off. With a sullen hiss its movement ceased.

In desperation I selected the international distress frequency. I knew that a call on this frequency would bring instant help.

'May Day, May Day, May Day,' I called. The silence was deafening. I tried the second radio. Again no reply. Chris's face had a far-away expression.

'If we are near Paris they won't want us bumping into their aircraft; let's try to call them,' I suggested. We did not have the correct crystal but we did have one for the secondary frequency of Paris Orly.

There was an immediate response.

'Lima Romeo what is your present position?' came a reassuring voice.

'Fathead,' yelled Chris. 'If we knew where we were we wouldn't need his help. I reckon we are near Bretigny.'

'We estimate approaching Bretigny at 4,000 feet,' I replied.

'Lima Romeo for identification turn right heading – zero six zero,' he instructed. 'Do you wish to divert to Orly?'

'Affirmative.'

Concentrating like mad I made the right turn.

'Lima Romeo, you are identified on the turn; this will be a ground controlled radar approach.'

With eyes glued to the instruments we followed his directions making a series of turns and descending through layer after layer of cloud. Inside the aircraft nobody spoke.

*Harold and Chris. Two relieved pilots at Orly, Paris.*

At 500 ft. we were still in cloud.

'Lima Romeo, you are now one mile from touchdown your height should be 300 ft...'

'I've got the lights!' Chris yelled interrupting the controller.

The cloud base was just under 300 ft. and we landed on the misty, soaking wet runway.

A 'Follow Me' car arrived and took us to a parking spot away from the terminal.

'Welcome to Paris,' grinned John.

'So you had a leetle trouble with the weather?' smiled the Air Traffic Officer.

'We certainly had an unpleasant surprise. Thank you very much for allowing us to land,' was about all I could manage to say.

Orly was the main airfield of Paris and extremely busy.

'I'm not sure how to calculate your landing fee,' continued the Air Traffic Officer.

He seemed almost pleased to see us. However, a strange sinking feeling had entered my stomach. We had spent all our money in Lyon, little thinking we would be landing again in France. He must have noticed my discomfort.

'Will that be a problem?' he asked.

'Actually, we didn't expect to land again in France and we don't have a great deal of money between us.'

'Have you been far?'

I told him.

'*Mon Dieu!* I think we will overlook the landing fee, better go to Meteo and see what is happening. Do you have enough money for something to eat?'

At least we could afford coffee and cake. The balding Met. Officer wore an enormous pair of thick spectacles. Around him teleprinters clattered a discordant symphony of information.

'The front passed across your route but moved far more slowly than we originally thought. You flew right into it Wait two to three hours and you will have clear weather with just the occasional shower.'

Outside the rain was now drumming on the windows. We lingered over our coffee and cake, attracting curious but friendly stares from the aircrews bustling around us.

'It's clearing,' called Phil.

Sure enough the rain had stopped and patches of blue could be seen. Within a surprisingly short time the sky was almost clear. The Air Traffic Officer showed us the route to take out of Orly that went around the south of Paris until Versailles, and then north-west along our outbound route to

*Four survivors reach Gatwick*
*(left to right, Chris, John, Harold and Phil).*

Gatwick. What a difference ten days had made to our navigational skills ! Our stress free and accurate journey back was a joy and we happily landed at Gatwick to clear customs. All that was left the final fifteen minute leg to Biggin Hill. A great cheer went up when Biggin answered our radio call.

'Call downwind runway 29,' came our instruction for our last landing.

We were all so relaxed, too much so. I joined for a standard left hand circuit.

'Look out,' cried Chris, pointing at an oncoming aircraft.

'That idiot's flying the wrong way round the circuit.' I took avoiding action.

'There's another one,' called John, pointing ahead.

'Fancy finding two nitwits like that on the same circuit,' I replied.

Then the penny dropped. Biggin Hill operated a non-standard right hand circuit on that runway. It was us who were flying in the wrong direction! I discreetly turned away from the airfield and rejoined the circuit a few minutes later. Whether or not anyone noticed I don't know, nothing was ever said. Peter Chinn and Tiny Marshall were on the tarmac to greet us as we taxied in. Several club members were also in attendance.

'Do you remember the last time you had a reception like this?' smiled Peter.

'I don't think I'll ever forget it!' I replied. 'But on that occasion none of you were smiling.'

We were treated like conquering heroes. Of course, we were happy to be back and relieved as well but we were saddened to bid farewell to our faithful Prentice which had carried us faultlessly for the entire journey.

'Shall we have an annual reunion with a short flight?' asked Phil.

It seemed like a good idea but at that time we had all flown quite enough. Sadly we were not to be reunited with Lima Romeo as she was lost with all on board some months later in the hills of Scotland.

Later that year I was awarded the Harris Challenge Trophy for the Best Navigational Flight of 1960. Of course, my brave and supportive friends deserved to share the award. Sir Francis Chichester, the renowned helmsman, made the presentation. Among many other achievements Sir Francis had sailed single-handed around the world. Far from the large tub-thumping extrovert that I expected, I found a medium built man with a quiet unassuming manner who

was eminently approachable. He was extremely interested in
our trip. It seemed to be a good opportunity to compare
nautical and aerial navigation. Instead, I found a man who
had a deep understanding of aviation.

'Finding an island in the middle of an ocean at the extreme
limit of your machine's range can be a bit tricky,' he smiled.

'How can a sailing boat have a limited range, apart from
food and water for the crew?' I asked with surprise.

'Of course you're right, I was referring to a light aircraft. I
used to do a spot of flying myself before the war.'

Sir Francis' comments prompted me to look further into
his 'spot of flying'. I discovered that Sir Francis had been an
outstanding pilot of the pre-war era who had made an epic
flight from London to New Zealand in a de Havilland Moth.
He had worked out a method of finding distant landmarks
by deliberately flying one side of the track so he knew which
way to turn after the allotted time. I learnt how, on entering
a valley in New Zealand, the turbulence was so severe that it
threw the little Moth onto its back. Undaunted Sir Francis
recovered the machine to level flight and tried again. This
time he got through. Reading of his feats of navigation,
endurance and courage, was an education, but I learnt more
than that. Outstanding pilots are not to be found propping
up bars recounting apocryphal exploits. They are normally
quietly spoken, unassuming, and always keen to help others.

CHAPTER 13

# Power Without Propellers

A FEW DECADES and several thousand flying hours later I was to be reminded that age and experience are not absolute guarantees against mishaps. A modicum of pressure and a degree of impatience can still be a lethal cocktail. In this instance the pressure stemmed from time constraints. I had been obliged to leave the renewal of my twin-engine jet rating until the last possible moment. Without the renewal certificate I could not fly the jet. I planned a morning test in the USA and a return flight to the UK the same afternoon – not much time for delays!

She sat there gleaming in the morning Florida sun. Rather more than twenty years old, this Citation twin jet was to be my mount for my examination, and what a little beauty she seemed to be. New leather seats with their inimitable odour of opulence complemented the fresh paintwork, new carpet and a highly polished cocktail cabinet. What more could a fellow want? At the back of my mind was the niggling thought that I had been very silly in leaving my renewal to the last possible moment but I at least felt happy that the machine that had been rented for me was in such splendid condition.

The restoration work, however, had stopped short of the cockpit, which had the original, somewhat dated, equipment, although it looked perfectly reasonable. The weather was fine, too fine in fact because it was already baking hot and it was still early in the morning. Then I noticed that there were no headsets, nor any checklists, but I did have a set that I had brought with me for a slightly larger model. A friendly face appeared at the pilot's widow.

'We're gonna fix up the external power,' he said, 'so you can run the air-conditioning and get the cabin real cool.'

'Many thanks,' I grinned, as I realised I was already perspiring freely in the 30°C temperature and the 'greenhouse' effect of sitting behind the large windscreen.

The additional air-conditioning unit produced a small gale but not much cooling; nevertheless when the main air-conditioning unit came on when the engines were started I was sure we would be comfortable.

Meanwhile I had to set about calculating the engine power settings, the rotation speed, the climb and approach speeds for our weight and for the ambient temperature. With a light load of fuel and just two people on board this little beauty was going to go like a rocket.

'Got the keys?' I asked the ground staff.

'Sorry, they are not in the flight office,' came the reply, 'but you don't really need them.'

Technically speaking they were correct. You don't need an ignition key to fly a jet aircraft, and once the cabin door is unlocked there is little to stop you operating it. The only trouble was that you need a key to open the external hatches and to check that all the essential reservoirs are full. If one of the hatches were closed but not actually locked this would trigger the warning on the dashboard to say that there was a door unlocked. Effectively it meant that we would not know if any other hatch or door came unlocked, but I was confident that I would examine each one meticulously as part of the pre-flight checks.

It was getting hotter and my exuberance was beginning to wane, but only slightly. My examiner, Burt, was one of the most experienced training captains in the United States, being a licensed examiner for Flight Engineers and Captains on every commercial aircraft in existence and quite a few antique ones as well. My examination of the aircraft systems and my understanding of it were concise but amazingly searching and as we wandered out to the Citation I explained the problems I had encountered.

'Are you happy to fly?' he said.

'Certainly,' I replied.

'Then it's OK with me.'

We walked around the aircraft together while he quizzed me on all the various components that needed to be examined.

'Here, let me show you a problem with a Citation door,' he said. He manipulated the door until it looked closed and then gave it a thump and the door flew open

'See what I mean,' he grinned. If you had been standing near the door in flight it would have been goodbye.

'Now let me see you close the door.' I closed the door. He gave it a hard thump. This time the door did not budge but Burt's palm started bleeding.

'This is not a very good start,' I thought.

We seated ourselves in the baking cockpit. I started going through a checklist.

'Start up the right,' yelled Burt. 'Let's get some cooling working.'

Obediently I pressed the right-hand starter button and the

familiar whine commenced. I stared in disbelief as all the engine gauges went berserk, and hurriedly shut the engine down.

'That's interesting,' I muttered.

'OK, we'll let it cool down, start the left,' said Burt.

The left engine started normally and I was just going through the sequence when I heard a yell from Burt.

'My ears, my ears, shut it down!' I looked at the cabin pressure gauge and realised that there was a major problem with the pressurisation unit, which had already over-pressurised the cabin on the ground. The day was not getting any better!

Instead of saying that this aircraft was not airworthy I suggested that as the test was to be conducted below 12,000 feet we could fly with the aircraft unpressurised. Burt agreed. The right engine now started normally, Burt briefed me on my tasks and I in turn agreed with him on the various duties that we would both carry out.

'You are to act as captain but in the event of a real emergency I take control,' Burt reminded me.

Both of us were now perspiring profusely and the taxiing checks revealed that neither the autopilot nor the yaw damper worked.

'You won't need those anyway on the test,' grunted Burt. 'Now let's have fun!' He smiled at me. 'Let's get this baby into the air.'

That was easier said than done, as the airfield was extremely busy. I briefed Burt on his duties. 'Call "Airspeed alive", 70 knots, V1 and Rotate. Please help with the power setting on the initial roll.'

The sun beat down mercilessly and after an eternity we lined up for take-off. We began to accelerate, Burt set the power and my airspeed indicator came off the stops, but no word from Burt. As a hint I called 'Airspeed alive': silence from my right. We seemed to be accelerating quickly, but because of the high temperature (or so I thought) my airspeed was increasing at a snail's pace. Then to my horror my indicator smartly fell back to zero.

'Lost airspeed indicator,' I called. 'Abort!' and reached towards the throttles.

'Go,' said Burt, but no V calls followed.

By now there was no possibility of stopping and the rapidly approaching houses at the end of the runway helped me to decide to rotate at roughly the same time as Burt reached towards the control column with the same thought in mind. Then my training kicked in.

'Positive rate of climb, gear up,' I called. Burt obediently retraced the gear.

'Immediate left turn,' called Burt. 'There's another airfield ahead.'

As I commenced the climbing turn my stomach seemed to turn over. My altimeter was still reading zero! A glance across to Burt's instruments revealed even worse news. His airspeed indicator was reading zero and his altimeter minus 50 feet. Between us we had no pressure instruments. This was quite impossible as all the systems were duplicated or even quadrupled in some instances. A jet is no open cockpit biplane that could be flown by the feel of the wind or the noise from the bracing wires. This aircraft had to be flown by numbers and we had none.

Burt was now taking an active interest in the proceedings.

'Angle of attack,' I muttered. I looked at the gauge, only to discover that that it too wasn't working. Burt was fiddling with the GPS, trying to make it work, and an awful thought occurred. If he could obtain an altitude reading and a ground speed reading from it was he really going to make me complete the test under these impossible conditions? The GPS didn't work.

'What are your intentions, Skipper?' Burt calmly enquired at this stage.

'I think we should return to the field,' I replied, sick at the thought of having missed my deadline when I should have been concentrating on more important issues like staying alive.

'We're coming back,' announced Burt over the radio. Turning to me he said, 'Now I want you to intercept the ILS and make an approach down to decision height. You tell me when we reach it. The help I will give you is to suggest you put down landing flaps early so that you have a stabilised platform.'

Just flying by feel and attitude was very strange. Neither of us really knew at what speed we were travelling. There was no radar altimeter so decision height was going to be an educated guess but at least the weather was good. I managed to intercept the glide slope about five miles from the airfield and did my best to keep the needles crossed in an attitude that appeared normal. We seemed rather fast over the hedge, but who cared ? Touchdown was normal if somewhat fast, there was a faint squeal of protest from the tyres, and with some relief I brought the aircraft to a halt.

'Well,' said Burt. 'There are a few lessons to be learnt from that.'

He was certainly right.

★    ★    ★

Back in Europe and at another time it was nightfall and I was alone in the cockpit. The embers of a fiery sunset still provided light to our lofty perch at 41,000 ft. but beneath us it was already dark. To our right could be seen the wake of a ship, a mere speck, that appeared to be drawn to the dying sun like a bar to a magnet. Behind in the dusk lay Brindisi. Outside howled an unheard sub-arctic oxygenless hurricane, but inside, separated from it by a few inches of fuselage thickness, the passengers relaxed cocooned in luxury. In the quiet cockpit the electronic displays glowed silently providing up-to-date information of all the aircraft systems and functions. An autopilot linked to the computerised navigational system was flying the aircraft. Ahead lay the inky blackness of the Greek mountains. Even the harassed and hoarse voices of the overworked Greek controllers fell silent as their traffic went on its way allowing me to think back to earlier adventures. The Prentice laboriously crawling its way over mountainous terrain belonged to a bygone era and another world. Gone were the open cockpit biplanes, flying through railway stations, and the fear of untrained instrument flying in cloud. I thought of Chris, Phil, John and all my friends and adventures shared as the stars began to appear in the crystal clear heavens. My reverie was interrupted by a smell of perfume.

'May I sit in the co-pilot's seat?' enquired one of the passengers. 'Your friend is spending some time back in the cabin.'

I strapped her in, and demonstrated the emergency oxygen system. My companion gazed forward at the night sky ahead, breathing deeply as if to savour every sector of the amazing landscape that lay before us. Abruptly she turned towards me.

*Then…Chipmunk cockpit circa 1955 with instruments
similar to those of the World War II era.*

*Now…Raytheon Hawker 800XP:
Cockpit of a modern business jet.*

'What's changed since you learnt to fly?' she asked.

I hesitated, 'Automation, electronics and turbine power have changed the entire face of aviation. We now take for granted travel approaching the speed of sound, above the weather, and at the edges of the stratosphere.'

I thought for a moment before continuing, 'Perhaps it is more important to consider what has not changed. The freedom of the sky, the adventure, the beauty of the clouds and landscapes and the never ending challenges have not altered. When they do it will be time for me to give it up.'

*Then: Luton Airport circa 1960. The Club House (bottom centre)
and a grass area adjacent to it were popular gathering points for
pilots and would-be aviators.*

*Now: Luton Airport 2004. A thriving international airport.*

# Index

173